MICROFILM: THE LIBRARIANS' VIEW, 1976-77

BY PAULA DRANOV

OWLEDGE INDUSTRY PUBLICATIONS, IN
TE PLAINS, NEW YORK

Microfilm: The Librarians' View, 1976-77
   by Paula Dranov

Library of Congress Catalog Card No. 76-17481
ISBN   0-914236-05-9

Printed in the United States of America

Table of Contents

List of Tables

I

SUMMARY

It has been 40 years since libraries first began relying upon microfilm to resolve some very basic problems -- 40 years since decaying back files of the New York Times first were replaced by reels of 35mm film in compact boxes. The immediate advantages were obvious: libraries could have a permanent back file of the Times and save precious space in the bargain.

IMPETUS FOR MICROFORMS

Since then, microforms have been making deeper and deeper inroads into library collections. But over the years, the reasons why libraries have come to rely on microforms have changed. Although saving space and preservation are still important advantages, the overriding factor today is cost.

The rapid increase in the cost of books and journals in the past ten years has caused many institutions to take a second look at microforms as an alternative. Figures gathered by R.R. Bowker and reported in the "Bowker Annual of Library and Book Trade Information" and in Publishers Weekly show that between 1965 and 1975, the average price of a hardcover volume increased from $7.65 to $16.07, or 112%. This upward spiral was especially noticeable between 1973 and 1975, a time of rapid inflation in the economy, when per-volume prices jumped by 32%. Though library budgets have continued to climb steadily during this same period, an ever-shrinking portion of those budgets has gone for acquisition of new materials. Figures in the "Bowker Annual" estimate that for college and university libraries, spending on books and other materials fell from 38.4% of the budget in 1970 to 34.4% in 1974.

Under these circumstances, librarians have been more willing to listen to the argument that they should step up

their acquisition of materials on microform (though in
actual practice purchases of microforms have kept pace with,
not exceeded, overall budget growth). The needs are especially acute for college, university,and special libraries
that must maintain the integrity of research collections.
Many of the last group, serving corporations and government
agencies, have begun to rely on microforms as the most
economical means of providing (and storing) an accelerating
flow of information.

MAJOR CONCLUSIONS

    This state of the art report is based on a review of
the literature, a mail survey of libraries, and telephone
interviews with librarians conducted between June 1975 and
April 1976 by Knowledge Industry Publications. The inquiry
has yielded five major conclusions about microform usage in
libraries today.

    . The amount of material available on microfilm has
increased steadily, as have libraries' purchases, but there
is still no shift to acquire original publications, such
as new books and journals, on microform.

    . Microfiche has emerged to challenge 35mm rollfilm
as a significant format. Most librarians are resigned to
the coexistence of several different formats, though they
would like to see more standardization. The micro-opaque
card is widely disliked and appears to be on the way out,
while none of the high-reduction "ultrafiche" formats has
made great headway.

    . Microform reading equipment and associated hard-
ware are still serious obstacles to more widespread use
of the medium. The evaluation and maintenance of equipment, as well as patron education in its use, are constant
headaches. Reliable reader/printers and equipment that
can handle several different formats are the most universal
needs.

    . Uncertainty over the suitability of non-silver
films, vesicular or diazo, is hampering wider use of microforms by libraries. Librarians would like to take advantage
of the lower cost of the non-silver films, but are confused
as to whether such films are durable enough.

    . Use of microfilm for administrative and record-
keeping functions is a still new and promising area for

libraries. The most intriguing application is for catalogs produced by computer-output-microfilm (COM) techniques.

TYPE OF MICROPUBLICATIONS

Today's library users have grown to expect to find
back issues of newspapers, periodicals, and journals on
microform rather than in bound volumes. In addition, libraries have been purchasing several other types of material
on microform. They include:

--large research collections which otherwise would be
unavailable;

--doctoral dissertations;

--government reports including those of the National
Technical Information Service (NTIS), a Department of Com-
merce agency which makes public all unclassified reports
produced by a variety of governmental branches, and those
distributed by the Educational Resources Information Cen-
ter (ERIC).

In addition, the Government Printing Office in 1976
completed a four-month pilot program to test the effective-
ness of using microfiche rather than hard copy for distribution to depository libraries of the massive Code of Federal
Regulations. The fiche were distributed to 33 of the 1186
depository libraries the GPO serves. Following an economic
analysis and pending the approval of the Joint Committee on
Printing, the GPO will begin giving depository libraries a
choice of fiche or hard copy.

Despite the fact that the federal government is the
largest micropublisher in the world, the groundswell of
information that has been available on microforms for the
past ten years has been due largely to the efforts of commercial micropublishers who realized early in the game that
there was a market among academic libraries for research
material that was not available to them in hard copy. These
micropublishers constituted a new industry quite distinct
from the traditional publishers of books, periodicals, and
newspapers. Today, there are upwards of 200 such publishers
offering microforms for commercial sale. Some are small and
highly specialized but the largest ones, including Xerox/
University Microfilms, Bell & Howell Micro Photo Division,
Readex Microprint, the New York Times/Microfilming Corp. of
America, and Princeton Microfilm Corp. have extensive and
varied micropublishing programs.

Nevertheless, the overwhelming majority of microforms are republications of material originally issued in book or journal form. Whether because libraries are unwilling to acquire original material in microform, or because publishers are unwilling to take the risk of issuing it in that form, or for both reasons, the fact remains that acquisition of microforms is still largely relegated to supplementary, not primary, materials. (A relatively recent development has been the simultaneous publication of scholarly journals in microform as well as in hard copy. Pergamon Press, a leading publisher of primary journals, launched a simultaneous publication program in January 1976.

FORMATS

Initially all micropublications were available only in one format, 35mm microfilm. Later, in the 1940s, came the micro-opaque card still produced by Readex Microprint. It wasn't until the mid 1960s that microfiche became a common format. Today, fiche seems to be catching up with 35mm film as the predominant microformat, while micro-opaques appear to be on their way out.

Until recently, most material available on microfilm was simply a miniaturized version of the hard copy from which it was reprinted. But as micropublishers devised larger and larger packages of information -- packages that represented many volumes of hard copy -- librarians began complaining that micropublishers were simply photographing and miniaturizing the hard copy with little regard for the needs of the ultimate user. Technicians with no library experience were making such mistakes as photographing books in Arabic and Hebrew backwards. Demands began to mount for more careful preparation and arrangement of the documents and the creation of accompanying bibliographic tools including catalog cards, indexes, and abstracts.

Of necessity, meeting these demands meant higher costs for the micropublishers -- costs that were passed on to their customers, the libraries. Today, while most micropublishers agree that there is an acute need for more and better bibliographic tools to accompany large microform collections, they are dubious about the willingness of libraries to pay for them.

From a library point of view, the substitution of microforms for hard copy presents some hidden costs not readily apparent when the price of a micropublication is compared to the price of the equivalent information in hard copy. In addition to the microform itself, the library must invest in equipment so that the micropublications can be read. And, it must set aside space to house that equipment and to accommodate users comfortably. The cost of a microform program has led some librarians to wonder if the savings microforms offer are worth it. Some are even doubtful about the space savings microforms make possible, given the fact that microform reading rooms take up considerable blocks of space.

HARDWARE AND READER RESISTANCE

Even more problems are presented by microform hardware -- the readers and reader/printers. Librarians have long been aware that they do not constitute a large enough body of customers for equipment manufacturers to design hardware specifically for the library environment. Complaints have ranged from those related to human engineering -- that viewing screens are too high or angled improperly to permit comfortable reading -- to those related to durability -- that most equipment isn't suitable for the heavy use it gets in the library and for the inadvertent mistreatment it receives from inexperienced and technologically unsophisticated users. The demand for paper copies of microform material is especially heavy in research-oriented libraries, and complaints about the unreliability of reader/printers and the poor copies they produce are a constant headache.

The development of low cost lap microfiche readers has enabled many libraries to begin to satisfy users who have been frustrated by the fact that they must sit in the library to use microfilm for research while equivalent material in hard copy can be circulated. Although very few libraries now circulate microforms and lend readers, the development of new and better lap readers will increase the availability of these services. Furthermore, as users begin to purchase their own personal, portable readers, libraries' microfiche duplication and circulation programs will increase. A growing number of libraries are equipped with on-site film duplicators that allow them to provide patrons with a microfiche copy to go. The cost of furnishing such fiche duplicates is low, provided that copyright clearances can be worked out.   .

A very real obstacle to the expansion of library microfilm programs has been the resistance of patrons to the use of microform material. Without a doubt this resistance can be traced to some of the problems mentioned above: the inadequacy of hardware, the lack of bibliographic access to some large microform collections, and the fact that with few exceptions, libraries do not circulate microforms and lend readers. To those factors must be added a psychological one that cannot be ignored: microforms are not books and cannot be treated as such.

Readers cannot flip through the pages or refer from one section to another as they can with books. No matter how badly a reader needs information contained on microfilm, the impersonality of the medium itself becomes a barrier to use.

Ironically, this attitude toward microforms stems to a large degree from librarians themselves. For all the needs microforms fulfill, librarians frequently have made their use more difficult and more inconvenient than it actually is. This negative attitude has been communicated unconsciously to library patrons and reflected in the relegation of microforms and microform reading equipment to out-of-the-way locations in the library, locations that frequently are unattractive enough to discourage patrons from returning. And it is reflected in the poor maintenance of microform reading equipment and the impatience of library staff members with the questions of patrons who don't know how to use the equipment.

FILM PROBLEMS AND OUTLOOK

Predictions are difficult to make in such a rapidly changing field. Only a few forecasts can be advanced with reasonable certainty. Micropublishers see continued rising prices for microforms, in response to increases in the cost of silver used in the film itself and to the mounting demands from librarians for more and better bibliographic controls. In an effort to head off some of the most drastic of the cost increases, micropublishers have been attempting to convince librarians that silver halide film -- now considered the only type acceptable for archival purposes and the only one for which national testing standards have been established -- should be replaced with vesicular film which is cheaper.

But for the most part, librarians have been unwilling to take a chance on the substitution. This reluctance stems to a large extent from an American Library Association (ALA) recommendation that until national standards are established for vesicular and diazo films, libraries specify that they will accept microforms only on silver film. As far as bibliographic controls are concerned, micropublishers have made clear that they can supply these tools only by passing the considerable costs along to libraries. While specific cost increases are difficult to project, at least one survey has forecast that they will rise to the point that by 1980 libraries will be spending 60% more on microforms than they were in 1972-73 and receiving 0.5% fewer units.

Although costs are likely to restrict the expansion of libraries' microform collections, other uses of microfilm within the library are expected to increase. The development of computer-output-microfilm (COM) has had a considerable impact on libraries.

The most obvious advantage of this new technology is as a substitute for card and book catalogs and as a cheaper alternative to on-line catalogs. While only a handful of libraries have made the switch to COM, an increasing number are contemplating such a move. Here, again, cost is the overriding factor: COM-produced catalogs are cheaper than maintaining and updating extensive card catalogs, much less expensive than computer-produced book catalogs, and offer the additional advantage of faster production. Using conventional typesetting, printing, and binding techniques, it may take months to print a book catalog from computer tape, whereas only a few days are required to produce the same catalog on microfilm.

MICROFILM FOR INTERNAL USE

For some time now, libraries have been relying on microfilm for internal uses such as circulation systems and books-in-process lists. Recordkeeping chores have been simplified by reducing mountains of paper to handfuls of microfiche. Here, savings are apparent not only in terms of convenience and easy access to information but in costs: film for recordkeeping does not have to be of archival quality. The cheaper vesicular and diazo films are perfectly acceptable for these purposes, especially since the microforms are disposed of periodically (a books-in-process list on microfiche has no use once the books no longer are in process.) Although COM catalogs must be of good enough quality to be easily read, they, too, are disposed of periodically as catalogs are updated, usually every six to eight weeks. For this reason, the expensive silver halide film is not required -- it would be a waste of money to use it for catalogs and records that are replaced frequently.

Another internal use of microfilm, though this has acquisition functions as well, is the preservation of information contained in deteriorating books or back issues of periodicals. Although some large libraries do have their own reprography departments to do microfilming of books which are crumbling, for the most part libraries must rely on commercial micropublishers to supply microfilm copies of books in need of restoration and rebinding. Although the cost of a microform copy may be higher than the cost of binding, it generally is much lower than restoration costs (deacidifying, repairing, laminating, and rebinding combined). To date, no reliable figures have been develped on the extent of substitution of microfilm copies for binding in library preservation programs.

Both the COM-produced catalogs and the preservation of deteriorating materials are illustrations of microfilm applications that may have received too little attention in the past but that, with improvements in micrographics technology, can be expected to be of growing importance to libraries in the future.

II

LIBRARY MICROFORMS: AN OVERVIEW

Since 1936 when the New York Times first appeared on microfilm, libraries have been receiving an ever-growing flow of new and better microforms. And they have learned that microforms offer far more than the space-saving and preservation advantages that had been so obvious when microfilm was introduced. They found that it was sometimes cheaper to buy microforms than the equivalent information in hard copy. Moreover, certain specialized research collections could be made available on microform whereas publication in hard copy would have been economically impossible. Of course, this proliferation of microforms has meant that libraries must have machines that make it possible to read them, machines that are less than perfect and which create their own kind of problems. For 30 years, however, as long as microforms constituted only a very tiny percentage of a library's total holdings, these problems were regarded as little more than a minor irritation.

By the mid 1960s there were big changes afoot. In addition to 35mm rollfilm, aperture cards, or micro-opaques, there were other newer microforms: 16mm film, microfiche, and ultrafiche. The most significant new format was microfiche, which has gained rapid user acceptance in the past ten years. It was perhaps inevitable that more microforms meant more problems for libraries. Broadly speaking, these fall into two areas: the first concerns the technological aspects of microforms and the equipment needed to read them; the second concerns micro-publications, the ever-increasing volume of information being made available on microforms. This chapter treats both.

THE TECHNOLOGY: FORMATS AND EQUIPMENT

Microfilm reels today are available in 35mm, 16mm, and 8mm widths. The most commonly used in libraries is the 35mm film which is available either on reels or in cartridges.

For the most part, it is used to reproduce newspapers or other large documents reduced from one-tenth to one-eighteenth of their original size. In general, a news-paper page 15 inches wide by 24 inches long fits on 35mm rollfilm if reduced to 1/18th of its original size.

Banks and business have been the heaviest users of 16mm roll microfilm, but in the past ten years it has been increasingly used for the micropublication of journals at reduction rates of 18X to 24X and, lately, for library records produced on computer-output-microfilm (COM). Whether or not libraries will continue to use 16mm microfilm remains an open question. The latest purchasing criteria for the California State Universities and Colleges specified that libraries in that system "will phase out all purchases of roll microfilm which appear on 16mm film and limit pur-chases of such microfilm materials to those which are available on 35mm film."

By and large, libraries have tended to prefer 35mm film not only for standardization of services and supplies, but also because of the higher quality and larger image it makes possible. For the most part, 8mm film has been by-passed by libraries and restricted to very limited use in business and industry.

The "fiche" in the word microfiche is a French word that translates as "card," and that's just what a microfiche is -- usually a 4x6-inch or 3x5-inch transparent card con-taining rows and columns of separate frames, each frame representing a single image, usually a page of print reduced to from 1/18th to 1/250th of its original size. Any image reduced to less than 1/90th of its original size is classi-fied as ultrafiche. Using a high enough reduction ratio, a single 4x6 fiche can accommodate up to 14,000 or more "pages" with each tiny image constituting one page. Today, most microfiche are produced in accordance with standards promulgated by the National Micrographics Association (NMA) and since adopted by the Committee on Scientific and Techni-cal Information (COSATI) of the Executive Office of the President. They provide for placing 98 letter-size pages reduced to 1/24th of their original size (24X) on a 4x6-inch microfiche. The pages are arranged on the fiche in a grid pattern consisting of 14 rows across and seven rows down.

To read a microfiche or ultrafiche, the transparent card is slipped between two flat glass plates on the reading machine. Below the bottom plate is a grid that corresponds to the placement of images on the fiche itself.

For all their current popularity, microfiche are rather new on the library scene. They were preceded by a similar "unitized" format -- the micro-opaque which is similar to the microfiche except that it must be read via reflected rather than transmitted light. While micro-opaques offer the advantage of easy handling, the format is on the wane largely because the associated reading and duplicating equipment never has been regarded as particularly efficient. Indeed, a survey of librarians undertaken in connection with this report found that micro-opaque readers ranked high on the list of "microform troubles." The 1975 CSUC standards reflected the mounting prejudice against this medium, stating emphatically that, "The libraries will abandon the purchase of micro-opaque cards and microprint except where necessary to complete sets to support academic programs because reliable and inexpensive printers for these materials are not available."

The microform least used by libraries in general is the aperture card -- electronic accounting machine cards into which a film frame is inset. They have been most extensively used for the reproduction of drawings and design documents in the engineering field.

In summary, then, libraries today are concerned primarily with two types of microforms: 35mm rollfilm and the NMA standard microfiche. The selection of readers for these two formats -- and for the others necessary to some collections -- is a problem that clearly frustrates many librarians. An oft-heard complaint is that, "There are no microform readers suitable to the library."

Howard White, editor of Library Technology Reports, the American Library Association (ALA) publication that periodically surveys the equipment scene and reports on microform readers and reader/printers it considers suitable for library use, confirms that the complaint is a perennial one. A few firms, such as Information Design, Inc. and Library Microfilms & Materials Co., have attempted to specialize in equipment for library use, but most microfilm equipment is still intended for a broad range of customers, with libraries constituting only one part. Libraries just aren't big enough customers compared with business and government organizations which buy many more readers and reader/printers.

In an attempt to determine exactly what librarians do want in a microform reader, Robert A. Morgan, president of R.A. Morgan Co. which evaluates microform reading equipment for LTR, had librarians "design" the ideal reader at the 1975

ALA meeting in San Francisco. The viewer had the following features: it could handle both fiche and rollfilm, could go from 16X to 48X in magnification, would have an angle of inclination of the screen of 45 degrees, a 1000-hour lamp, a screen size of 15x15 inches and an overall size of 20x20 -- small enough to be moved by one person. Other desired features were a quiet fan cooling system and image rotation of 180 degrees.

To illustrate the cost of all these library-tailored features, Morgan estimated such a machine would have to sell for $3000. The audience was willing to pay about $600. Librarians "want the moon but they don't want to pay for it," White reflected after the meeting.

A November 1975 LTR survey listed 150 models of readers and reader/printers considered suitable for the library. Of these, 12 were designed to handle two different formats, that is both film and fiche. LTR steers clear of making specific product recommendations on the theory that no one reader can be adapted to all situations. "It depends on the microform collection," White explains, "and on intangibles like the availability of service representatives. All we can do is test equipment and provide guidelines."

In July 1976, LTR will be joined by a new equipment reviewing guide, Micrographics Equipment Review to be published by Microform Review. In announcing the availability of the new service, Microform Review said it would be designed "to provide the decision-maker with all of the information needed for intelligent micrographics equipment purchasing decisions." Alan Meckler, publisher of Microform Review and MER, sees the new review as an adjunct to LTR. He calculates that about 35 new pieces of equipment come out every year for libraries and proposes to review 80% of them. Editor of the new publication will be consultant William R. Hawken.

MER's reviews will analyze the technical aspects of each piece of equipment and consider the clarity of operating instructions, ease of maintenance, availability of a manufacturer maintenance network, likely durability of the machine, and comparison (where possible) to similar equipment. LTR's reports usually cover the same ground.

These two publications offer libraries the only independent evaluation of microform reading equipment. The NMA has attempted to provide some orientation for libraries through a series of seminars instituted in 1973. Each year, the NMA sponsors four seminars, one offering an across the board introduction to micrographics, another providing a training workshop on inspection and quality control of microforms. Special additional sessions geared for librarians have been scheduled, but an NMA spokesman said recent ones have been cancelled owing to "lack of interest."

Relations between the library community and the NMA have been strained to say the least. In an effort to heighten awareness of library needs among manufacturers and to educate librarians about all aspects of micrographics, a Library Relations Committee was formed within the NMA in 1973. It was disbanded two years later with the chairman, Carl Spaulding of the Council of Library Resources, reporting that "...NMA officials have disregarded the commitment made to the library community."

COMPUTER-OUTPUT-MICROFILM (COM)

The most important hardware development in recent years has been in the area of computer-output-microfilm (COM), the means by which information contained on computer tape can be converted directly to microfilm. The most obvious application of this new technology in the library is as a means of producing catalogs. The procedure is as follows: machine-readable catalog data are put into a computer and new acquisitions are routinely added. At set intervals, a computer tape of the entire catalog is retrieved and sent to a service bureau for reproduction on either microfilm or microfiche. Less than four years ago, COM catalogs were a novelty to be found in only a handful of U.S. libraries. Today, however, interest is accelerating and the number of libraries turning to or considering COM increases steadily. The reasons are obvious:

. The elimination of the often unwieldy card catalog and the filing and cost problems of keeping it current.

. The ease and economy with which copies of the microform catalog can be distributed.

. The speed with which catalog formats can be revised quickly and cheaply in subsequent editions.

. The cost advantage COM catalogs offer over computer-produced book catalogs or even more expensive on-line catalogs.

Potential disadvantages are not so obvious and may be identified only after wider experience with COM catalogs.

Some that have been predicted include the queuing that could result if not enough viewing stations are available to permit convenient catalog consultation; the lack of standardization of page and record formats and of reduction ratios that could prove an impediment to the sale and exchange of COM catalogs; and the lack of availability of reader/printers to make possible the potential advantage of cheap and easy copying of complete bibliographies from COM catalogs.

The first significant application of COM technology to library catalogs came not in the United States but in Great Britain. As far back as 1972, Francis F. Spreitzer of the University of Southern California at Los Angeles Library reported that enthusiastic public response had been found after COM-produced rollfilm catalogs were introduced in England. Both the Cornwall County Library and the Westminster City Library rated COM catalogs as good alternatives to paper printouts which they had found to be too expensive.

The most comprehensive survey of COM catalog use in the United States was carried out in 1975 by Kenneth J. Bierman of the Tucson (Arizona) Public Library. The purpose of Bierman's study, which was underwritten by the Council on Library Resources, was to determine the "current state of planning and implementation for computer-generated replacements for the card catalog (book catalog, microimage catalog, on-line catalog) for large collections (250,000 titles or more) and selected smaller libraries (less than 250,000 titles) that had actually implemented an alternative form of catalog."

Bierman found that, "All the microimage catalogs are less than five years old, and the majority are less than two years old. Computer-output-microfilm (COM) catalogs are becoming popular; they can be produced for a fraction of the cost of a corresponding printed book catalog and in a fraction of the time (weekend turnaround time for a complete cumulation is possible)."

Although no large libraries have microimage catalogs replacing the main public card catalog, both the New York State Library and the University of British Columbia have announced plans to close their card catalogs and implement microimage catalogs. Of the ten libraries that had COM catalogs in use, most reported that user acceptance was high. Of the ten, two were public libraries (Tulsa City-County Library, Oklahoma and Marin County, California) which had not had the catalogs in operation long enough to judge user acceptance. Three were special libraries -- including Lockheed in California and Boeing in Washington State -- which rated user acceptance as high. Five were academic libraries which also found good user acceptance, although one, the University of Texas/Permian Basin, had turned up some complaints that the catalog was "hard on the eyes" and that machines were difficult to use. Florida Technical University and two other University of Texas campuses are among other academic libraries with COM catalogs.

Since the Bierman study was completed, the Baltimore Public Library has instituted a COM catalog in all of its branches. After determining the cost advantages, Director Charles Robinson reported that there was little public reaction. "Librarians are very concerned about catalogs," he explained. "People are not." The new catalog was put into service in October 1975 and is updated every time the library adds 2500 titles or about every two or three months. Problems to date have fallen into two areas:

. Equipment breakdown: "That's about as expected," Robinson said. "Machines break down....I don't care who makes them, they do. And these get very heavy use." Baltimore's reader is supplied by Auto-Graphics. Though the library considered Information Design's ROM II, the advantage of Auto-Graphics, according to Robinson, is that a single firm supplies the hardware and processes the information and the file itself.

. The quality of the microfilm: The catalog file itself uses vesicular film which has the advantage, according to Robinson, of being cheaper and of working in the reader better than silver or diazo films because of its harder surface. However, he did complain that most COM producers aren't used to making high quality masters, a necessity when microfilm gets the constant heavy use it does as a catalog. "People have to see clearly," he adds, "and that's a different requirement. Usually, COM is produced for maximum storage rather than heavy use."

Robinson believes more and more libraries will go in for COM catalogs "because of the cost," an opinion shared by Bierman who predicts that for the next 25 years large libraries will have two catalogs: "a frozen retrospective catalog in card or microimage form and an on-going catalog in machine-readable form."

In January 1976, seven public libraries in the Raisin Valley System in Michigan began converting to a COM catalog

and installed some 30 readers provided by Information
Design. The system calculates that quarterly updates of
the COM catalog will cost $5300, compared to $11,000 for
a book catalog and $24,000 for maintaining the present
card catalogs. The Prince Gilbert Library at the Georgia
Institute of Technology, which has been using a COM-produced
catalog since 1971, says the annual cost is $3500 to $4000
vs. a minimum of $8000 for a card catalog.

Other libraries considering the adoption of COM catalogs include such public library systems as Fairfax County,
Virginia and Orange County, California. Despite savings
from COM, Bierman still foresaw no wholesale switch from
the card catalog by the nation's large libraries until the
Library of Congress decides what direction it will take.
Indeed, many large libraries contacted by Bierman in the
course of his studies stated that, "Any major change from
a card catalog toward an automated catalog would and should
wait for LC to take the leadership role." To date, the
Library of Congress has only suggested the possibility of
closing its card catalogs by 1980 and beginning on-line,
printed book, and microimage catalogs then.

In summary, Bierman found that despite the growing
interest among large libraries in automated alternatives
to card catalogs, no major change would take place until
at least 1985. For the most part, he predicted, alternatives to card catalogs among large libraries will be on-line
catalogs supplemented with hard copy catalogs in card and/
or microimage and/or printed book form.

"Exclusively printed book catalogs for large collections will not be acceptable because they are slow to
appear and expensive to print and cumulate," he reported.
"Exclusively microimage catalogs for large collections
will not be acceptable because of the user interface and
acceptance problems and because they offer no significant
improvement over card catalogs in improved searching capability. Because of the automated catalog's ability to
be responsive to change, large libraries will be in a
constant state of alternative 'mixes' of on-line, hard copy,
and microimage catalogs to meet changing situations, needs,
and financial conditions in the future."

COM has other applications in the library apart from
the card catalog. For instance, the New York Public Library maintains its authority file on COM as well as its
books-in-process list.

MICROPUBLICATIONS

As the amount and type of information available on microforms multiplies, problems relating to their acquisition and use have come to the forefront. Broadly speaking, these fall into three distinct areas: (1) film; (2) formats; and (3) bibliographic control. Of the three, the most currently controversial is the film issue.

Film

Three types of light sensitive materials are currently used for the production of microforms, only one of which is considered suitable for archival purposes. This one, silver halide, is the most expensive type available and is used for the master, the original microfilm copy of a document, and the distribution copies that micropublishers sell to libraries.

The other two types of film, both widely used and both cheaper than silver film, are diazo and vesicular. Diazo films are sensitive to ultraviolet light. They are composed of diazonium salts mixed with chemical couplers and acid stabilizers. Although diazo film is said to be less susceptible to damage and scratching and less easily affected by heat than silver film, it has yet to be certified for archival quality, and testing standards for it have not yet been developed. A subcommittee of the American National Standards Institute (ANSI) has been working since 1971 to develop tests for both diazo and vesicular film, but no definitive word on their suitability for archival materials is expected for at least three years.

Vesicular film is the newest of the three types available. Like diazo film, it is sensitive to ultraviolet light. In fact, the name "vesicular" was chosen to describe the bubbles or "vesicles" formed by the action of ultraviolet light on the diazonium compounds in a crystalline plastic emulsion. By now, most librarians are familiar with the story of what happened when vesicular film produced by the Kalvar Co. of New Orleans, LA was used for microfilm copies of the New York Times. Some of the film was found to give off excessive amounts of hydrogen chloride gas under normal storage conditions -- gas that leaked through cardboard containers to corrode some of the metal filing cabinets in which the film reels were stored. Ultimately, after pressure on both the Times Company and the Kalvar Co., most of the defective film was replaced, also with vesicular film

unless the library specified that it would accept only
silver film. (Between 1967 and 1975 the Times was offered
only on silver film. In 1976, it began offering the option
of vesicular again and found that 80% of the subscribers
preferred this choice. Karl Horwitz of The New York Times/
Microfilming Corporation of America calls vesicular the
"film of the future.")

Since then proponents of vesicular film have been stepping up pressure to substitute it for silver halide in a
variety of micropublications. They argue that vesicular
film offers two important advantages: it is cheaper than
silver film and it is as durable for everyday use. Similar
claims have been made for diazo film. The controversy was
succinctly analyzed in 1975 by Great Britain's National Reprographic Centre for documentation (NRCd). In a "Proposal to
Investigate Methods of Determining the Storage Life of Diazo
and Vesicular Microforms," the NRCd stated the problem as
follows:

"General industrial and personal experience has shown
that diazo images can deteriorate in as short a time as five
years while other diazo films are in good condition after
some three times this figure...."

As far as vesicular life is concerned, the NRCd proposal
had this to say: "It is known that heat will cause vesicular
images to disappear, whether this is applied during storage
or during use....It would appear that vesicular images are
otherwise highly stable...."

The NRCd proposed a five-month project "to find the
factors which cause deterioration of these materials and
thus to make recommendations for storage and use which will
enhance their useful life."

To date, neither the NRCd study nor the work of the ANSI
is near completion. Nevertheless, more and more micropublishers are attempting to convince librarians that the lower
cost and ease of duplication of these two types of film merit
their substitution for silver halide. One of the most out-
spoken proponents of this view is Richard McDonald, vice
president for marketing of Bell & Howell's Micro Photo Di- -
vision. "We feel bullish about vesicular film," he states
bluntly. "We feel it will have a big place in the future.
We've done extensive testing and the problems of the past,
I think, are solved."

McDonald advocates substitution of vesicular for silver
halide in use copies of micropublications. "Our masters are

on silver halide and are archivally stored," he explains.
"Should a library need a replacement for a vesicular use
copy, it can always get one. A company like Bell & Howell
stands behind its products. We feel the use of vesicular
film is a way to reduce our costs and to pass that savings
along to libraries. The cost of silver these days is out
of sight and is continuing to increase. We've had to raise
our prices because of the rising price of silver, although
I don't think we've been out of line in our increases."

McDonald predicts a "substantial switch" to vesicular
film in the next year or so, a view not necessarily shared
by other micropublishers. A spokesman for Xerox/University
Microfilms indicated that most libraries are sticking with
silver film and that while research continues on the durability and life expectancy of the other two types, no switch
is in the works.

Harold Harsh, president of the Kalvar Co. contends that
vesicular film is more practical for libraries that do not
store their microforms under the archival conditions pre-
scribed by the ANSI. He views the attempt to convince librarians to stick with silver until ANSI standards are
developed for vesicular film as a "flim flam." If you use
film, it will wear out, Harsh argues -- any film. Under
normal conditions, he maintains, vesicular film is as durable as silver halide "if not more so."

Suggestions that vesicular film be substituted for
silver halide in library micropublications have been termed
an "ominous trend" by Microform Review editor Allen B. Veaner.
And in 1975, two ALA committees, the Standards Committee of
the Reproduction of Library Materials Section and the Micropublishing Committee of the Resource Section issued a strongly
worded recommendation "that libraries buy for their permanent
collections only microforms (such as silver halide film) for
which standards for archival permanence have been established
by recognized standards organizations." Veaner, who has continued to wage a vehement editorial campaign against the purchase of other than silver film, raises the question of what
would happen should a company which promises to replace any
vesicular microform that didn't stand up under library use
be sold to another company, abandon its micropublishing program, or simply go out of business. While Veaner does concede
that non-silver films do have some advantages over silver
halide, he asserts that, "The fact remains there are as yet
no national standards for testing the durability of non-silver
images or the efficacy of their processing. Therefore, the
burden of proof for the durability of non-silver materials is
upon the producer and not on the library....Libraries may wish

to consider the incorporation of a specification in their
purchase orders and contracts requiring the sole use of
materials for which national standards have been published."

The Archivist of the United States, Dr. James B. Rhoads,
has taken a similar position. In a letter quoted in the
March 1976 Journal of Micrographics regarding standards for
diazo and vesicular films, Rhoads contends that any material
approved for "permanent record filming" must be "equal to or
better than the present materials that have been certified
for permanent record use." In other words, "Permanent or
archival record film can be defined as any film that is equal
to or better than silver film."

Formats

If the film controversy remains unresolved, so does
another regarding the proliferation of new and different
microformats and the equally new and different reading machines they require. To date, there doesn't appear to be
any overall trend among libraries toward one format over
another. Indeed, many librarians voice indifference to the
format -- what they care about is acquiring the information,
no matter whether it is on film or fiche. Nevertheless,
Richard McDonald at Bell & Howell says he sees a strong preference for fiche for two reasons: (1) delivery time is
usually faster than for rollfilm and (2) the cost of rollfilm
readers is substantially higher than the cost of fiche readers.
The opposite trend was reported by a Xerox/University Microfilm spokesman who said that fiche enthusiasts usually are
among the microform uninitiated -- the librarians buying
microforms for the first time. They're attracted, he said,
because fiche seems more convenient to use and easier to in-
sert into the reader. In time, he adds, many fiche fans
become converts to 35mm film, saying "by far" the use of
film exceeds that of fiche in libraries today.

In the late 1960s and early 1970s, several ultrafiche
or high reduction microfiche formats made their appearance
in collections aimed solely at library customers. E.g.,
Library Resources, Inc., an Encyclopaedia Britannica affiliate, announced a "microbook" program consisting of thousands
of volumes, filmed at a 55X to 90X reduction ratio and distributed on 3x5-inch fiche.

Those programs increased the range of materials available on microfilm, but the appearance of ultrafiche and of
microforms issued in varying reduction ratios has led to a
demand for standardization -- a plaintive cry of "Enough!"

from librarians with budget problems who simply can't afford
new readers for every new microformat that comes along. However, more recently, librarians have increasingly recognized
that the microformat must be suited to the material being
filmed -- that no one type of microform can accommodate periodicals, newspapers, and books of varying page size, quality,
etc.

The dilemma was analyzed in a 1973 Library Journal
article by micrographics consultant William R. Hawken. His
contention was that, "The search for a universal microform
was abandoned years ago. The search for universal compatibi-
lity between microforms and their associated hardware must
be abandoned." Arguing for "systems instead of standards,"
Hawken likened microforms to trucks and contended that, "No
one 'standard' truck could efficiently perform all of the
different conveyance functions required." Small pickup
trucks had one function, huge tractor trailer trucks another,
he pointed out, given the variety of transportation and delivery needs that trucks serve. As with microforms, the
different "standards" were simply a recognition of the different purposes to which the vehicle was being put.

Imposing standards now on microforms while the "technology pot is indeed boiling" would impede progress, Hawken
wrote. Forceful though these arguments may be, it is the
rare library that has unlimited resources to keep pace with
the technology. And apt as the truck analogy may seem, it
also can be argued that no one business needs all kinds of
trucks. Libraries certainly can't be faulted for attempting
to control costs by insisting that the microforms they purchase be compatible with available hardware.

The California standards promulated in 1974 were an
attempt to do just that. The standards were divided into
two general areas, the first relating to the human factors
to be considered in the purchase of microform reading
equipment and encompassing factors ranging from the instructions, controls, and image of readers to screen size,
and reading room environment. The second part set limits
on the acquisition of microforms and microform equipment,
specifying that the libraries would restrict purchase of
reading equipment "to that which is designed primarily to
operate between 16X and 24X." It instructed libraries to
"avoid the acquisition of microform materials produced at
higher reduction ratios than 48X until such time as indus-
try-wide standard reduction ratios are established and
acceptable to the Library Directors."

Where a choice of microforms exist, the standards stated, the libraries will "purchase the materials in microfiche and/or 35mm rollfilm depending upon the content of the material filmed, provided that the microfiche shall not be larger than 4x10 in size." As mentioned earlier (see page 11), the standards required that the libraries abandon the purchase of micro-opaque cards and microprint except where necessary to support academic programs. In establishing this rule, the CSUC committee stated that it would use every opportunity "to urge micropublishers who produce micro-opaque materials to make these materials available in microfiche form."

Today, most micropublishers selling to the library market adhere to the NMA standard microfiche -- a 4x6 card with 98 images reduced to 24X or 1/24th of the original page size.

Acquisitions

Once a format is decided on, the purchase is made and the film is delivered, libraries are still up against the problem of confirming that they got what they paid for. Virtually no library has the staff or facilities to do more than run a spot check of microforms to ensure that new acquisitions are in good, readable condition. For the most part, librarians report that defects in micropublications tend to be detected only when a patron is using the material and discovers that some parts of it are either missing, out of focus, poorly photographed, or otherwise unreadable.

In an attempt to alert librarians to the problems they may encounter in their microform acquisition programs, Allen Veaner enumerated the potential dangers in a 1968 Choice article. That piece has since been expanded by Veaner into "The Evaluation of Micropublications: A Handbook for Librarians," published by the Library Technology Program of the American Library Association and now the bible of many librarians as they set about microform acquisitions. Essentially, Veaner cautions librarians to determine in advance what they can expect to receive as a result of a given order. Questions that should be foremost in the mind of a purchasing librarian concern the microformat, the film type, reduction ratios, finding aids -- both internal and external -- financing arrangements, replacement policy, etc.

Much of his advice has since been incorporated into the American National Standard for the Advertising of Micropublications issued by the American National Standards Institute on April 14, 1975. The standard is aimed at spelling

out for micropublishers "the elements which will provide
in their advertising the basis for a critical evaluation
of their published products by prospective purchasers."

The information included in advertising and promo-
tional materials should encompass the discount price (if
any), prices of individual titles in a collection, the
actual or scheduled publication date, the size of the microform and the range of reduction ratios used, the polarity
(positive or negative), the film type, whether or not ANSI,
NMA, or Library of Congress standards have been followed.
In addition, the standard recommends a description of the
size of the particular microform collection (pages, volumes,
titles, and microform units included) and of any retrieval
aids provided.

Elementary as some of these specifications may seem,
the standards are a response to some very real problems
encountered by librarians venturing for the first time into
the world of micropublications. Some of those problems, to
be sure, stem from the naivete of librarians who simply were
not adequately prepared to evaluate the ever-growing volume
of micropublications. Others stem from some outright shady
practices by an unethical minority of micropublishers. So
extreme have some abuses been that the ALA Bookdealer-Library
Relations Committee has twice issued warnings about objection-
able business practices. The most recent, distributed in
December 1975, cautioned libraries that one or more micropublishers "may be securing copies of materials already in
microform, reproducing them, and reselling the microforms
at higher costs."

In one instance, an 84-reel microform project available
at $1260 from the originating agency was offered by another
vendor at $2200. (Although unethical, the practices are not
illegal, the Bookdealer-Library Relations Committee reported.
The micropublishers in question had been careful to confine
their holdings to materials that are in the public domain,
not copyrighted, or for which a valid copyright is not held
in the United States.)

The Bookdealer-Library Relations Committee is in the
process of drafting guidelines for the ordering of micropublications expected to be ready for distribution in the
fall of 1977. Essentially, the guidelines will offer a run-
down of what librarians should be aware of in ordering micropublications and will suggest resources for librarians to
consult in order to learn more about micrographics.

As far as the micropublications themselves are concerned, there are several authoritative sources librarians
can check to determine what is available. A new book,
"Microforms in Libraries: A Reader" by Albert James Diaz,
contains a comprehensive listing. Among the most important
are "The Guide to Microforms in Print," an annual, cumulative list of materials available on microfilm, microfiche,
and micro-opaque from U.S. publishers, and a companion
volume, "Subject Guide to Microforms in Print." These two
publications have recently been acquired by Microform
Review, which itself publishes an annual cumulation of
non-U.S. microforms in its "International Microforms in
Print: A Guide to Microforms of Non-United States Micropublishers." Included are monographs, journals, newspapers,
and government publications.

The Library of Congress issues the annual, non-cumula-
tive but comprehensive "National Register of Microform Masters,"
a listing of master microforms from which duplicate copies are
available and master microforms housed in a temperature-
controlled, fire-proof space and owned by a non-profit institution. The function of the "Register" is to record only
those masters held for the specific purpose of making duplicates. Other important sources listed by Diaz include the
"National Union Catalog," Updata's "Microform Volume I" and
"Microform Reference Volume II," both of which list micropublications that can be purchased through Updata, and the
"Micropublisher's Trade List Annual" (Microform Review).
Publishers' catalogs are another obvious source of information as is the Microform Clearinghouse Bulletin, issued
irregularly by the Library of Congress as a supplement to the
LC Information Bulletin.

Since its inception in 1972, Microform Review and its
spin-off publications -- "Microforms in Libraries," "International Microforms in Print," and the upcoming Micrographics
Equipment Review -- have found a ready audience among librarians. Until its appearance, there had been no publication
providing reviews of major new microform collections as they
were issued, so librarians had to depend on micropublishers'
catalogs and announcement bulletins for this information.

That Microform Review filled a void is obvious both in
the response of libraries and librarians to its publications
and the success of its First Annual Library Microform Conference in New York in October 1975. The two-day session

jointly sponsored by two ALA divisions attracted nearly 400 librarians from all over the country. The second annual conference is scheduled for Atlanta in October 1976.

Though libraries have complained there is inadequate notification about materials on microfilm, they have been fairly passive about demanding that more original materials be published in this medium. There are exceptions, of course, such as the Government Printing Office's decision to begin micropublication of certain government documents after ascertaining that many depository libraries would prefer this format. Nevertheless, growth of original publishing in microform has been very slow.

The University of Toronto Press, which for a time had planned to issue all monographs simultaneously on microfiche and in hard copy, has abandoned this program because demand for the microfiche was very limited. Pergamon Press, which began simultaneous publication of various of its journals in 1976, says response to the program has not been overwhelming. However, Edward Gray, president of Pergamon's parent company, Microforms International Marketing Co., professes to see a "clear trend" among libraries toward fiche for their journal subscriptions.

LIBRARY HOLDINGS

Despite the expanding interest in and knowledge of microforms, these materials still represent only a relatively small portion of library holdings and are an equally small item in library budgets. Nor is it certain that expenditures on microforms have been growing at a faster rate than overall library acquisitions budgets. To date there have been no authoritative estimates of how much libraries are spending on microforms or of how large a proportion of library holdings is represented by microforms. The latest attempt to determine what libraries are now spending and to project what they will spend in the future was made in a survey by consultant John Dessauer for Publishers Weekly. Dessauer's conclusions were presented in an article "Library Acquisitions -- A Look into the Future" in the June 16, 1975 issue. They subsequently were discussed by a panel of experts assembled by the ALA Research Committee and the Library Materials Price Index Committee at the ALA 1975 San Francisco conference.

Dessauer based his microform findings on reports gathered from librarians. His figures on book expenditures were compiled from a variety of sources including PW price statistics;

TABLE II-1: Percent of Total Materials Budget for All Libraries by Type of Materials and Type of Library*

Library Type	Percentage of Total Library Spending Contributed By:		Percentage of Total Micro-form Spending Contributed By:		Percentage of Total Audio-Visual Spending Contributed By:		Percentage of Total Binding Spending Contributed By:		Percentage of Total Periodical Spending Contributed By:		Percentage of Total Book Spending Contributed By:	
	1972-1973	1978-1979	1972-1973	1978-1979	1972-1973	1978-1979	1972-1973	1978-1979	1972-1973	1978-1979	1972-1973	1978-1979
Academic	33%	33%	46%	45%	10%	11%	55%	55%	53%	51%	31%	30%
Public	19	21	14	16	9	12	15	16	8	8	27	31
Special	16	19	28	30	5	6	27	28	29	33	14	16
School	32	27	12	9	77	71	2	2	9	7	28	23
Total All Libraries in Millions of $			$41.9	67.1	195.3	266.9	41.2	63.6	200	339.5	500	741.3
Total % of all Materials for All Libraries			4.3%	4.5	20.0	18.1	4.2	4.3	20.4	23.0	57.1	50.1

*Calculated on the basis of Dessauer's "Estimated Comparative Materials Expenditures by U.S. Libraries 1972-73, 1978-79," Publishers Weekly, June 16, 1975.

surveys by the Association of American Publishers; price indexes prepared for the "Bowker Annual"; Fred C. Lynden's "Survey of Library Materials Expenditures at Stanford University Libraries" (October 1974); and interviews with librarians. Periodical figures were based on Library Journal statistics; indexes in the "Bowker Annual" and Stanford survey; "Periodical Prices," a three-year comparative study by F.F. Clasquin, Library Journal, Oct. 1, 1974; and interviews with librarians.

Dessauer estimated that $42 million was spent by librarians on microforms in 1972-73 and projected that $67 million would be spent in 1978-79. Although those figures represent an increase of 60.1% in library expenditures for microforms, Dessauer calculated that the amount would represent a drop rather than an increase in the actual number of microform units acquired. He estimated, for example, that while academic libraries will be spending about $30.5 million on microforms in 1978-79, this money will buy 4.3% fewer microform units than they were able to purchase with expenditures totalling $19.3 million in 1972-73.

He also projected that while the same institutions will be spending almost 50% more on books in 1978-79 than they did in 1972-73, they will receive 13.5% fewer volumes. For periodicals and binding, the forecast was also for higher spending but fewer physical units.

Dessauer forecast that special and public libraries will be spending about 75% more for microforms, enabling them to increase unit purchases over 1972-73. School libraries, which according to Dessauer's figures will be spending only 11% more on microforms in 1978-79 than in 1972-73, will be adding 32% fewer units.

All told, Dessauer projected that by 1978-79 all libraries will be purchasing 0.5% fewer microforms than they did in 1972-73, although their overall expenditures will be up slightly more than 60%. In reviewing Dessauer's figures, Frances Spigai of Central Oregon State College, made the following observations:

(1) Libraries apparently are not purchasing microforms as a substitute for binding as evidenced by the estimate that in 1978-79 there will be 2.1% fewer units bound constrasted with 0.5% fewer microforms -- a difference too slight to indicate a trend.

(2)   The discrepancy between 6.4% fewer periodicals and 0.5% fewer microforms could mean that a larger part of the microform budget is being spent on sets of monographs rather than back sets of periodicals.

(3)   Dessauer's forecast that the units of microforms purchased will drop doesn't square with figures from the Association of Research Libraries showing that in 1973-74, members' microform holdings were up 13% while hard copy volume count rose by only 4%.   However, it would seem that Dessauer's estimate that academic libraries will be spending more but getting 13.5% fewer books for their money by 1978-79 supports the trend reported by the ARL.

Francis Spreitzer of the University of Southern California Library had something to say on the question of microform sets and their place in library microform acquisitions after a survey of 60 libraries in 1974.   He concluded that while microform acquisitions in general were on an upward curve, the very large, multi-thousand volume sets might be on the way out simply because the discretionary funds for them have dried up.

MICROFORM USE

For many librarians,an especially frustrating aspect of their investment in microforms is the existence of two major obstacles to microform use.   The first concerns access, a two-fold problem stemming from the fact that most libraries do not have the staff or facilities to catalog all incoming microforms and the failure of many micropublishers to provide what librarians consider to be adequate bibliographic tools -- indexes, catalog cards, and the like.   The second stumbling block is that of reader resistance -- the reluctance on the part of library patrons to grapple with what many feel is a much too complicated way to acquire information.   Often this resistance problem is compounded by the failure of libraries to make the use of microforms and microform reading equipment convenient and comfortable.

Bibliographic control

Speaking at the First Annual Library Microform Conference sponsored by Microform Review, Robert Grey Cole, assistant dean of Library Services at Southern Illinois University, identified the establishment of bibliographic control as "the major problem in microforms in libraries." Grey takes the position that microforms should be as

accessible as paper documents and entered in library catalogs the same way, a point of view disputed by some librarians.

He traced the current confusion about the proper
bibliographic handling of microforms back to their first
appearance in libraries when they often were shunted off
into their own obscure corner simply because there was no
official rule for cataloging them. As a result, library
patrons had no way of knowing what was available and whole
collections fell into disuse. Even today, cataloging practices are uneven, as indicated by results of the survey
described in Chapter III. And while librarians often were
at fault for not tackling the cataloging of microforms
when it was still manageable, micropublishers also were
to blame, said Cole, for not providing adequate indexes
or for charging more for indexing than libraries could afford to pay.

At present, according to Cole, the bibliographic control problem can be considered critical, while efforts to
resolve it are rudimentary at best. Indeed, E. Dale Cluff,
head of the Library Media Services Department at the University of Utah's Marriott Library, reported in the October
1975 issue of Microform Review that, "Very little is being
done on a national coordinated basis to assist in the
bibliographic access of microform sets." Basing his conclusions on a survey of how academic libraries were indexing large, multi-volume microform sets, Cluff found that
most libraries "are handling major microform sets on an ad
hoc basis. No hard and fast rule guides the cataloging
and classifying of these materials." Cluff has proposed
an 18-month study to determine how best to approach the
bibliographic control question.

Another source of bibliographic development for microforms could be the Advisory Group on National Bibliographic
Control sponsored by the National Science Foundation, the
National Commission on Libraries and Information Science,
and the Council on Library Resources. The advisory group,
which held its first meeting in April 1974, has noted the
need for "a more coherent national bibliographic system."
Any national system of coordinated bibliographic files,
the group said, should be in machine-readable form and con-
tain records providing for the unique identification of
each item and listing appropriate locations of each. But
so far, the group has only established two working parties,
neither dealing with microforms: one covers formats for
journal articles and technical reports; the other, bibliographic name authority files.

Another tentative move toward determining the extent of microform cataloging in the U.S. today was undertaken in 1975 by New York METRO Reference and Research Libraries. It surveyed 35 libraries, a combination of Association of Research Library (ARL) members, and METRO members. It has mailed two questionnaires to libraries taking part in the survey, but expects to report no results until 1977.

Despite intense interest in the subject, little action has been taken even within the ALA. However, a session on bibliographic control of microforms is planned for the 1977 conference in Detroit. Some librarians also look to the Library of Congress or the Anglo-American Catalog Rules Revision Committee for more leadership in cataloging micro-forms.

Addressing the issue from a micropublisher's point of view, Richard McDonald of Bell & Howell said that while bibliographic controls are necessary and while Bell and Howell strives to provide them, he is dubious about whether libraries are willing to pay for them "because the cost is tremendous." Costs of providing bibliographic controls for research collections microfilmed 20 or 30 years ago were simply too high, though micropublishers have done retro-spective indexes for newspapers like the Washington Post and the Wall Street Journal.

Since the cost of indexing and cataloging is related to the complexity of the subject matter, micropublishers are hesitant to estimate just how much the cost of a col-lection goes up when extensive bibliographic tools accompany it. But the cost of cataloging and indexing tools, along with lack of bibliographic standards for microforms, are hampering access to microform collection.

READER RESISTANCE

Ever since microforms came into general library use, librarians have been reporting that patrons don't like them. In fact, they say,when told that information is available only on microform, many researchers simply abandon pursuit. In the early years of microforms, the reluctance to use them could be easily understood: unwieldy, unreliable readers, bad film with fuzzy or out of focus images, com-plaints that reading microfilm is hard on the eyes, that it isn't comfortable, that note-taking is difficult, that copying facilities are either unavailable or provide poor quality duplicates. In his 1969 user survey of microfiche

use ("Microfiche 1969 -- A User Survey"), Harold Wooster
garnered comments like this one: "Everything about microfiche is marvelous -- except reading it." Another user
told Wooster that microfiche is an "information burial
system." A 1971 study by James P. Kottenstette and K.
Anne Daily ("An Investigation of the Environment for Educational Microform Utilization, Phase II") focused on
student use of microform in the classroom. Reactions here
were just as unfavorable: "Destroy it." "Give it to IBM
so the computers can read in their spare time." "Discard
it."

Indeed, Francis Spreitzer found in his 1974 study
of microforms in 60 libraries throughout the U.S. that
user resistance was understandable in view of the unsatis-
factory conditions which persist in many libraries, even
though better equipment has become available. He took
librarians and micropublishers to task, laying the blame
for such resistance as might exist on their doorsteps.
Spreitzer said that less than 10% of the libraries he
visited had microform reading rooms he would rate as good.
Most were located in unattractive quarters in inconvenient
areas of the library with inadequate light and cramped
writing space, and were supplied with machines that weren't
kept in working order. And, he said in a private communi-
cation, micropublishers compound these problems with in-
sensitive formatting and a generally unimaginative transfer
of information into a very different medium. Moreover, libraries often fail to tell patrons that microforms are
available.

Spreitzer isn't the only micrographics expert who
holds librarians responsible for the user resistance problem. Others note that many libraries simply do not extend
themselves where microforms are concerned: instructions
on the use of machines may be unavailable or incomprehen-
sibly technical. Rather than explain and demonstrate the
use of the equipment to inexperienced patrons, harassed
staffers sometimes brusquely thread the microfilm or in-
sert the fiche themselves, leaving the user no more the
wiser and certainly no more comfortable about using microforms.

Relatively few libraries are new enough to have
specially designed microform reading rooms, but those that
do report that user reaction is positive (see Chapter IV).
In general, librarians say, the younger the users, the
more receptive the attitude toward microforms. Older patrons, particularly faculty members accustomed to taking
their research materials home with them and those people
who wear bifocals, seem to display the strongest resistance

to microform use. One librarian hazarded a guess that students entering college in the 1970s were so used to hardware in school that microforms are accepted as just another educational toy. Older faculty members, on the other hand, are simply not accustomed to audiovisual and library technology and find it difficult to make the transition.

Aside from these emotional factors, all of the problems discussed above -- equipment, film quality, the lack of standard formats and bibliographic control -- combine to frustrate user and librarian alike. Certainly there appears to be a rising awareness in the library community of the myriad problems relating to microform equipment, acquisition, and use. And certainly librarians have been the target of an expanding body of literature designed to keep them abreast of developments in the field.

The following two chapters are designed to shed some light on how libraries are coping with microforms today. Chapter III presents the results of a survey of 157 libraries aimed at identifying any emerging trends, preferences, or crises. Chapter IV is based on a series of informal interviews with librarians in an attempt to learn how they're handling microforms on a day-to-day practical basis.

III

A SURVEY OF LIBRARIAN EXPERIENCE WITH MICROFILM

For all the discussion and controversy generated by the expanding use of microforms, few attempts have been made to identify which problems loom largest in the eyes of individual librarians. In an effort to remedy this situation, a survey was conducted in June 1975 of the subscribers to Advanced Technology/Libraries, a monthly newsletter published by Knowledge Industry Publications. A total of 800 two-page questionnaires were mailed and returns were received from 157 libraries. Each respondent was asked to describe itself as an academic, public, school, or special library. In tabulating the responses, the category into which each library fell was taken into consideration. Thus, the results demonstrate, to an extent, the problems with microforms and their use encountered by these different types of libraries.

Although responses to each of the questions will be reviewed in detail below and illustrated by tables drawn from the questionnaires, a few broad conclusions can be stated at this point. For the most part, libraries were concerned primarily with the quality of the equipment they possessed. Here, the most severe problems related to the quality of micro-opaque readers, although it should be noted that relatively few institutions had such equipment. Those libraries with the largest problems in this area were those serving academic communities. (Of the 66 academic libraries, 30% of the respondents rated their problems with micro-opaque readers as large -- a hefty number considering that 14 of the 66 respondents said the question did not apply to them, presumably because they had no such equipment.)

A large majority of all respondents voiced some dissatisfaction with the quality of microfilm reader/printers. Fully one-third said that they had experienced occasional problems in this area, while more than a third categorized their problems here as either large or constant but not large.

The maintenance of microform equipment also was a major source of concern. More than one-third of the total respondents said they had occasional maintenance problems, while another third said they had either large or constant but not large problems in this area.

Fourth on the list of major problems were three items: microform equipment selection, microform reading area design or improvement, and multiple reduction ratios. Of least concern were the questions of microform circulation, microform acquisition, and problems relating to suitable containers, file cabinets and the like,and to the complexity of microform equipment.

In general, academic and public libraries were concerned primarily with equipment problems while special libraries identified their main problems as relating to multiple reduction ratios, microform quality, microform use, microform quality control, and the design or improvement of the reading area.

EQUIPMENT PROBLEMS

The first section of the survey sought to determine the extent of librarians' problems with microform equipment. Respondents were asked to classify their problems as one of the following: (1) large; (2) constant but not large; (3) occasional; (4) rare; (5) none; (6) not applicable. In tabulating the responses, a seventh category was added: no response.

The first question concerned the extent to which selection of microform equipment is a problem. Here, 53 of the 157 respondents, or 33.7%, deemed it an occasional problem. Another 13.4% viewed selection as a large problem (though for academic libraries, this percentage was 21%, compared to only 5.8% for special libraries and 13.6% for public libraries). Another 13.4% of the respondents indicated that equipment selection was a constant but not large problem. Here, the percentages were roughly equivalent among academic, special, and public libraries. As for equipment selection being rarely or never a problem, 31% of the respondents chose one of these two answers. (See Table III-1.)

Comments from the respondents on the problem of equipment selection are perhaps more illustrative of their difficulties than the tabulation of the responses. A few bluntly noted that equipment selection was no problem for them because no money was available to buy additional readers or reader/

TABLE III-1: Problems With Microform Equipment Selection

	(N)	Large	Constant but not large	Occasional	Rare	None	Not applicable	No response
Public	(22)	13.6%	13.6%	40.9%	9.1%	9.1%	--	13.6%
Academic	(66)	21.2	13.6	34.8	12.1	12.1	3.0%	3.0
Special	(69)	5.8	13.0	30.4	23.2	17.4	4.3	5.8
Total	(157) 100%	13.4%	13.4%	33.8%	16.6%	14.0%	3.2%	5.7%

printers. Others complained that,"The perfect machine for
the library environment has not yet been made." Another
put it this way: "Few if any pieces of equipment available
are intended to serve library (vs. business) needs and to
handle diverse reduction ratios." Several volunteered that
they are able to keep up with equipment developments through
literature, sales contacts, NMA dealers, and Library Technology Reports. One librarian complained that good film
readers are hard to find,while fiche equipment is more
readily available. Another voiced the opinion that there
is no adequate large-screen newspaper reader available.

Complexity and maintenance

Relatively few libraries reported large or constant but
not large problems arising from the complexity of microform
equipment. (Table III-2) In fact, half of all the respondents reported that they rarely or never encounter problems with complexity of equipment. Special libraries apparently have the least difficulty in this area; fewer than
a third had any problems. Academic libraries reported occasional problems in 36% of the cases, constant or large
problems in 17%.

More than half of the public libraries responding indicated that they had run into occasional problems stemming
from equipment complexity. One public library respondent
commented that "better directions" would alleviate some of
the difficulties due to complex equipment.

Academic librarians reported that users frequently had
trouble with the machines. One said pointedly that the
equipment presented "no problem for the staff" but added
that, "Users can't understand them." Another commented that
it was library policy to ask each user if he or she had op-
erated the equipment before and knew how to approach it.

Comments from special libraries indicated that they
took the question to mean whether the complexity of the
equipment had generated repair problems. One librarian
commented that the company had trained a staff repair group
while another said it dealt with problems arising from equipment complexity by reading the manual that came with the
machine and relying on an engineering technician when specific problems arose.

On maintenance, a third of the respondents indicated
either large or constant problems and another third cited
occasional problems. Academic libraries again reported

TABLE III-2: Problems With Complexity Of Equipment

	(N)	Large	Constant but not large	Occasional	Rare	None	Not applicable	No response
Public	(22)	4.5%	13.6%	54.5%	--	18.2%	4.5%	4.5%
Academic	(66)	6.1	10.6	36.4	28.8%	15.2	--	3.0
Special	(69)	1.4	11.6	15.9	47.8	17.4	2.8	2.8
Total	(157) 100%	3.8%	11.5%	30.0%	33.1%	16.6%	1.9%	3.1%

heavier problems than the other respondents: 53% said their
problems were either large or constant (Table III-3). In
the "occasional" group were half the public libraries and a
third of the academics. One respondent who indicated constant maintenance problems commented that, "Quality of hardware lags behind the quality and development of micropublications." Two respondents explained that a staff member
cleans and services the equipment regularly, but one of
these noted that a serviceman was called for breakdowns.
One librarian who described maintenance problems as occasional complained that service was not always available in the
event of breakdowns. One academic institution rated its
maintenance problems as large and specified that they particularly related to the 3M Reader/Printer.

On this issue special libraries commented that they relied upon service contracts for the maintenance of their
equipment. One respondent complained that, "Occasionally
repairs are impossible," and another who found constant maintenance problems stated that these were especially troublesome among older reader/printers.

Rollfilm and fiche readers

Asked to describe problems relating to the quality of
microfilm readers, nearly one-third responded that they
encountered occasional problems, while 51 of the 157 respondents said that they had rare or no problems stemming
from the quality of these readers (Table III-4). Only
25% reported large or constant problems. On this issue,
academic librarians again voiced the most complaints. One
who reported a constant but not large problem with the
quality of the library's microfilm reader repeated the frequent complaint that, "Most are not made for libraries."
Another who reported large problems in this area said that
the problems are usually "in design rather than sturdiness,"
while still another who reported occasional problems said
the microfilm readers were "hard to load" and added that
they are not consistent in loading method. A respondent
who reported large problems in this area voiced a preference for older models. A special librarian repeated the
common observation that library users who wear bifocals
complain about the quality of the microfilm readers.

About the same percentage of respondents -- 52 out of
157 -- reported occasional problems stemming from the quality of microfiche readers, but fewer than 20% had large
or constant problems. Here again, academic libraries were
most heavily represented -- 14 of the 28 respondents who

TABLE III-3: Problems With Equipment Maintenance

	(N)	Large	Constant but not large	Occasional	Rare	None	Not applicable	No response
Public	(22)	18.2%	18.2%	50.0%	4.5%	4.5%	--	4.5%
Academic	(66)	10.6	42.4	30.3	7.6	7.6	--	1.5
Special	(69)	4.3	15.9	37.7	18.8	15.9	4.3%	2.9
Total	(157) 100%	8.9%	27.4%	36.3%	12.1%	10.8%	1.9%	2.5%

TABLE III-4: Problems With Quality Of Microfilm Readers

	(N)	Large	Constant but not large	Occasional	Rare	None	Not applicable	No response
Public	(22)	13.6%	13.6%	31.8%	18.2%	13.6%	--	4.5%
Academic	(66)	12.1	24.2	34.8	10.6	13.6	4.5%	--
Special	(69)	7.2	7.2	27.5	30.4	10.1	13.0	4.3
Total	(157) 100%	10.2%	15.3%	31.2%	20.4%	12.1%	7.6%	2.5%

identified their problems with fiche readers as large or
constant   (Table III-5).   On this issue, however, the
special libraries were most specific about the problems
they encountered.   One reporting occasional problems
voiced the need for interchangeable lenses, while another
whose problems also were occasional noted that the most
frequent source of complaints about the quality of the
fiche readers were patrons who wear bifocals.   Still another commented that the library is "still looking for
the ideal cheap portable."

    The question relating to the problems with the qual-
ity of micro-opaque readers was described as "not applicable" by 69 of the 157 survey respondents, while
another 21 failed to respond at all to this question.
Of the 67 who deemed the question applicable, more than
half -- 38 respondents -- described their problems with
micro-opaque readers as constant or large   (Table III-
6).   Of these, 20 were academic libraries and on this
issue complaints ranged from "all are terrible" to "much
better machines required."   Two respondents stated that
micro-opaques are difficult to read and one explained
that in order to use the machines, the room had to be
darkened.   One of the respondents who reported large
problems said the machines in question were the Readex
Universal Microviewers and that the problems related to
focus and image quality.   Another library with large
problems in this area noted that, the "microcard was okay,"
but added that, "No satisfactory microprint-reader exists."
Two of the special libraries who responded to this question commented that their micro-opaque readers are rarely
used.

    For reader/printers, responses again showed con-
siderable dissatisfaction, and comments on this issue
reflected frequent breakdowns of the equipment.   Just
over 20% of the respondents (32 of the 157) reported
large problems with the reader/printers; another 18%
reported constant problems.   Here, again, the highest
percentage of problems were reported by academic libraries   (Table III-7).   One academic librarian who
reported large problems stated that, "We are looking for
improved equipment over the 3M 400" while another who
indicated only occasional problems complained that,
"Photographs do not reproduce well with our electro-
static printer (Xerox)."   A librarian who encounters
constant but not large problems with the reader/printer
stated that, "Constant maintenance is required in order

TABLE III-5: Problems With The Quality Of Microfiche Readers

	(N)	Large	Constant but not large	Occasional	Rare	None	Not applicable	No response
Public	(22)	4.5%	18.2%	27.3%	9.1%	13.6%	18.2%	9.1%
Academic	(66)	7.6	13.6	37.9	18.2	18.2	3.0	3.0
Special	(69)	8.7	4.3	30.4	31.9	13.0	4.3	7.2
Total	(157) 100%	7.6%	10.2%	33.1%	22.9%	14.6%	5.7%	5.7%

TABLE III-6: Problems With The Quality Of Micro-Opaque Readers

	(N)	Large	Constant but not large	Occasional	Rare	None	Not applicable	No response
Public	(22)	9.1%	4.5%	9.1%	--	--	54.5%	22.7%
Academic	(66)	30.3	13.6	18.2	3.0%	10.6%	21.2	3.0
Special	(69)	4.3	1.4	2.9	4.3	4.3	62.3	20.3
Total	(157) 100%	15.9%	7.0%	10.2%	3.2%	6.4%	43.9%	13.4%

TABLE III-7: Problems With The Quality Of Microform Reader/Printers

	(N)	Large	Constant but not large	Occasional	Rare	None	Not applicable	No response
Public	(22)	13.6%	31.8%	50.0%	--	4.5%	--	--
Academic	(66)	28.8	18.2	34.8	3.0%	7.6	6.1%	1.5%
Special	(69)	14.5	14.5	33.3	17.4	7.2	8.7	4.3
Total	(157) 100%	20.4%	18.5%	36.3%	8.9%	7.0%	6.4%	2.5%

to get decent copies." Another apparently frustrated librarian who runs into large problems with the reader/ printer commented succinctly that the machine (which was not identified) is "junk."

Complaints were less vociferous from public libraries, although one respondent who categorized his problems as large mentioned frequent breakdowns and noted that, "The copy of the positive is much better than the negative." Another who encountered only occasional problems mentioned that the copy is often unclear at the edges. In neither case was the machine in question identified.

One special librarian apparently had the opposite experience with the 3M 400 than the academic librarian quoted above. The special librarian stated that problems with the reader/printer were rare and commented that the institution was "still successfully using 3M 400." Another praised the 3M 500Cs as "very satisfactory," but there were some complaints from the special library group. One found that the reader/printer mechanism is "subject to temperature and humidity" and another commented that it could not get copies which can then be photocopied adequately. The bifocal problem was mentioned here again by a library which otherwise encountered reader/printer problems only rarely.

A related question concerned the extent of problems stemming from use of microform reader/printers (Table III-8). Here, only 20% reported large or constant problems, while 40% (62 of the 157) noted occasional problems. A total of 39 of the 157 said they rarely encountered problems related to reader/printer use, but comments from academic librarians indicated that in order to avoid problems, detailed instruction sheets must be attached to all machines and proper training of both the staff and library patrons is essential. One academic librarian who described use problems as occasional did say that the quality of copies sometimes presented a problem.

As far as public libraries were concerned, one responded that first time users of the machine frequently encounter problems,while another specified that simple instructions are required for proper use of the machines. Special librarians, too, pointed out the need for "constant education of users" and one librarian who reported occasional use problems noted that, "It is sometimes hard to convince others outside the department to use the machines."

TABLE III-8: Problems With The Use Of Microform Readers Or Reader/Printers

	(N)	Large	Constant but not large	Occasional	Rare	None	Not applicable	No response
Public	(22)	4.5%	22.7%	50.0%	18.2%	4.5%	--	--
Academic	(66)	7.6	22.7	36.4	18.2	3.0	3.0%	9.1%
Special	(69)	2.9	4.3	39.1	33.3	8.7	2.9	8.7
Total	(157) 100%	5.1%	14.6%	39.5%	24.8%	5.7%	2.5%	7.6%

FILM UTILIZATION AND PATRON PROBLEMS

The survey also attempted to determine whether librarians are encountering problems in adhering to standards for archival quality in storing their microforms (Table III-9). A total of 25 libraries ruled this question "not applicable" while another ten failed to respond to the question. Of the 122 who did respond, the largest number falling into any one category stated that they had no problems in this area. It is impossible to determine here if some of the respondents simply reported that they had no problems because they are not concerned with maintaining archival conditions.

From the comments received, it appeared that many of those responding "no problem" in fact did not even try to achieve archival standards. For example, one academic library which reported having no problem commented, "We don't try....Building is air conditioned." Another respondent who indicated no problem on the questionnaire added the comment, "We don't try....We have use copies only." And one special library reported having no problem and added that it has "no archival function." However, one academic library that reported occasional problems in maintaining archival storage conditions for microforms stated that, "The temperature in the storage room sometimes goes above optimum range." Another,complaining of large problems with storage,said these related to "lack of adequate temperature and humidity controls." A special library reporting constant but not large problems in this area conceded that storage,conditions were very poor but simply "not open to negotiation." Another special library that viewed this problem as constant but not large noted that, "Some of our microfiche are curling."

One public library expressed some frustration in this matter. And another which classified its storage problems as large added that it is "impossible to convince city hall" of the importance of maintaining better storage conditions. Still another,admitting to large problems in this area,said it had found damage to archival materials.

Integrating the collection

Responses to a question on the scope of problems related to the integration of the microform collection with the main collection also indicated that this was an issue many libraries have not yet attempted to resolve (Table III-10). Five failed to answer at all, 28 found the question not applicable, and 40 stated that they had no problem.

TABLE III-9: Problems Adhering To Standards For Archival Quality

	(N)	Large	Constant but not large	Occasional	Rare	None	Not applicable	No response
Public	(22)	18.2%	4.5%	22.7%	9.1%	22.7%	13.6%	9.1%
Academic	(66)	10.6	7.6	15.2	21.2	28.8	15.2	1.5
Special	(69)	5.8	8.7	18.8	11.6	27.5	17.4	10.1
Total	(157) 100%	9.6%	7.6%	17.8%	15.3%	27.4%	15.9%	6.4%

TABLE III-10: Problems Integrating Microform Collection With Main Collection

		Large	Constant but not large	Occasional	Rare	None	Not applicable	No response
Public	(22)	27.3%	13.6%	18.2%	9.1%	4.5%	22.7%	4.5%
Academic	(66)	13.6	12.1	15.2	9.1	25.8	24.2	--
Special	(69)	7.2	13.0	23.2	8.7	31.9	10.1	5.8
Total	(157) 100%	12.7%	12.7%	19.1%	8.9%	25.5%	17.8%	3.2%

Here, too, the fact that so many libraries fell into the no problem category may mean that many of them simply have not attempted the physical integration of microforms with the main collection. One public library that did not respond to the question commented that the two collections are separate, while another which viewed integration as a large problem said that the matter "needs study as the number of microforms grow." A public library encountering constant but not large problems with integration said that it had not determined "where to put...or how to handle" the microforms. A special library that said the question was not applicable added that it had not yet felt the need to integrate its collection. Another special library with occasional problems with integration identified these as the establishment of records to denote what is on film and also in hard copy. A special library admitting to a large problem concerning integration said it had been acquiring larger amounts of microforms in the past three years but still was not certain how to file them. The respondent added that any decision in the matter "must be based on frequency of use."

An academic library reporting only rare problems with integration said that it maintains a separate reading room on the main public floor of the library, while another which said its integration problems were large stipulated that this response related to both the physical integration of microforms with the main collection and the indexing of the microforms. An academic library reporting only occasional integration problems specified that the microforms in its collection are housed separately. It appears from the responses that most libraries have not completely integrated their microform collections with their main collections, although many are considering such a move. Judging from the preponderance of responses falling into the no problems, not applicable, and no response categories, it would appear that many libraries have simply postponed or do not intend integration of the two collections.

Relatively few libraries reported major problems relating to the storage of microforms in suitable containers or file cabinets. In fact, close to one-third -- 52 of the 157 respondents -- indicated that they had no problem at all in this area, while another 20% said such problems were rare (Table III-11). However, 23.6% reported occasional problems. One such respondent, a public library, indicated it anticipated more problems in the future, while an academic library with occasional problems relating to suitable

TABLE III-11: Problems Relating To Suitable Containers, File Cabinets, Etc.

	(N)	Large	Constant but not large	Occasional	Rare	None	Not applicable	No response
Public	(22)	9.1%	27.3%	22.7%	13.6%	22.7%	--	4.5%
Academic	(66)	10.6	9.1	27.3	15.2	37.9	--	--
Special	(69)	5.8	8.7	20.3	26.1	31.9	2.9%	4.3
Total	(157) 100%	8.3%	11.5%	23.6%	19.7%	33.1%	1.3%	2.5%

storage containers said its difficulties were primarily
budgetary. An academic library reporting large problems
in this area said it found containers "too expensive" and
noted that it is "trying to find alternatives." A special
library rating its difficulties as constant but not large
said it found the available containers "too expensive for
the quality." An academic librarian complained that the
containers are inefficiently designed for storage of a
large quantity of varying microform formats, while a public library with constant problems said its biggest concern
was finding the space to put the containers.

No definite pattern emerged from responses to a question concerning the design or improvement of microform
reading areas. About one-third said problems were constant or large, but another third said they had rare
problems or no problems at all (Table III-12). Among
the public libraries admitting to large problems was one
which conceded that its present arrangement was inflexible.
Yet another said there just wasn't space for adequate
microform reading room facilities in its 1905 building.
A special library with occasional problems said its main
concern was with overhead lighting and the glare it caused
on the surface of the screen. Another special library
which said it had no problems with the design or improvement of its reading room nevertheless conceded that, "Lighting in the area of the reader often makes microform difficult to read." Other special libraries said their major
problem was the need for more space, while one said it
was primarily concerned with two questions: how to mix
readers and files for easy use, and illumination require-
ments.

The light glare problem was mentioned by three academic libraries which described their reading area problems
as constant but not large, and others complained of over-
crowding and limited space. Comments on this issue were
more numerous than those volunteered on other subjects
covered by the questionnaire, indicating that librarians
are keenly aware of the relationship between microform
use and the environment in which they are made available.

Acquisitions and bibliographic control

Nearly a third of the libraries responding to the
survey said they had no problems with the acquisition of
microforms (Table III-13). Another 23.5% said they ran
into difficulties here only rarely,while 21% said they did
have some occasional problems. Only 15% had constant or

TABLE III-12: Problems With Microform Reading Area Design Or Improvement

	(N)	Large	Constant but not large	Occasional	Rare	None	Not applicable	No response
Public	(22)	36.4%	13.6%	13.6%	13.6%	13.6%	--	9.1%
Academic	(66)	18.2	16.7	27.3	10.6	22.7	3.0%	1.5
Special	(69)	11.6	13.0	31.9	18.8	15.9	5.8	2.9
Total	(157) 100%	17.8%	14.6%	27.4%	14.6%	18.5%	3.8%	3.2%

TABLE III-13: Problems With Microform Acquisition

	(N)	Large	Constant but not large	Occasional	Rare	None	Not applicable	No response
Public	(22)	--	4.5%	40.9%	18.2%	22.7%	4.5%	9.1%
Academic	(66)	3.0%	16.6	16.6	24.2	31.8	3.0	4.5
Special	(69)	4.3	8.7	18.8	24.6	33.3	5.8	4.3
Total	(157) 100%	3.2%	11.5%	21.0%	23.6%	31.2%	4.5%	5.1%

large problems. One academic library that reported constant but not large problems regarding acquisition complained that, "Not enough titles are available," but also
noted that, "Lack of funds is the main problem." Another
academic library with constant acquisition problems commented that the materials it needs are "not always available." Two others reporting only rare problems with
acquisition said that, "Most material comes on a standing
order basis and service has been good to date," while the
other said that acquisitions are handled by a separate
department and admitted that it "may not be aware of all
the problems."

A public library that said the acquisition problem
was "not applicable" explained that microforms are supplied by the state, while another public institution that
failed to respond directly to the question did comment
that its main problem was budgetary, the same problem
mentioned by a third public library that rated its acquisitions problem as large.

Special libraries reporting occasional problems with
acquisitions differed in their explanations of just what
those problems are. One said it found that, "Some titles
and/or years are not available in preferred formats," while
another complained of delays in purchasing from jobbers
and mentioned here the ERIC/EDRS and NTIS microforms.

The largest group of libraries -- 41.4% -- indicated
that they had only occasional problems with microform
quality, while 34% said they had none at all or rarely
encountered problems. Only 20% described their problems
as either constant or large   (Table III-14). Academic
libraries reporting occasional problems had two specific
complaints: that the quality of the microform was "frequently related to the quality of the original document";
and that problems occurred with "some foreign purchases."
One academic institution describing its quality problems
as constant said the film was "okay" but noted poor
resolution, while another stated that microforms are "not
standard enough."

A special library encountering occasional problems
hazarded a guess that, "The original may be the problem."
One special library with constant problems in this area
said they related to older titles where the "print is too
small." And another special library with constant problems mentioned that the New York Times on fiche "is impossible to print -- unclear."

TABLE III-14: Problems With Microform Quality

	(N)	Large	Constant but not large	Occasional	Rare	None	Not applicable	No response
Public	(22)	--	9.1%	45.5%	27.3%	9.1%	--	9.1%
Academic	(66)	4.5%	18.2	39.4	18.2	18.2	--	1.5
Special	(69)	5.8	14.5	42.0	23.2	5.8	7.2%	1.4
Total	(157) 100%	4.5%	15.3%	41.4%	21.7%	11.5%	3.2%	2.5%

A similar response was apparent on the question of
microform quality control: a third cited occasional
problems, 31% reported no or rare problems, only 18% said
their difficulties were either large or constant (Table
III-15). One special library which described its problems
as occasional noted that, "The best original is not always
available for filming," while another with occasional
problems voiced the opinion that, "ERIC is getting too
fussy; we prefer fuzzy information to no information at
all."

Two academic libraries mentioned the problem of bibliographic control in answering this question. One which
classified its quality control problems as occasional said
that, "Indexing and labeling are bad" and added that, "Some
foreign items are poor." Another, identifying its problems
here as constant but not large, said difficulties stemmed
from bibliographic controls, "both external and internal."

Respondents addressed the bibliographic control issue
more directly in replying to a question dealing with the
indexing and/or cataloging of microforms. Responses here
were fairly evenly divided, with 16% of the libraries
classifying their problems as large; 10% as constant but
not large; 20% as occasional; and 44% as rare or non-
existent (Table III-16).

One academic library with large problems here said
they were due largely to lack of personnel, while two
others with large problems mentioned microforms in sets
as particularly troublesome. One said the basic problem
was in the design of the publishers'sets, while another
said microforms in sets were "given second class treatment by both micropublishers and libraries." Comments
from special libraries reflected a lack of agreement on
this issue. One librarian who said his problems were
constant noted that there were no indexing or cataloging
standards yet for microforms and added, "Sure need it."
Five of the nine special libraries who volunteered comments said that they do not index or catalog microforms.
Only one, reporting rare problems in this area, noted
that, "Microforms are treated like books."

Responses to a question related to the problems of
integrating the microform index or catalog information
with the main catalog appeared to indicate that this is
not yet common practice. A total of 48 libraries reported
no problems in this area, while 26 said the question was

TABLE III-15: Problems With Microform Quality Control

	(N)	Large	Constant but not large	Occasional	Rare	None	Not applicable	No response
Public	(22)	4.5%	4.5%	31.8%	13.6%	9.1%	18.2%	18.2%
Academic	(66)	4.5	16.7	34.8	19.7	16.7	4.5	3.0
Special	(69)	7.2	10.1	29.0	20.3	7.2	21.7	4.3
Total	(157) 100%	5.7%	12.1%	31.8%	19.1%	11.5%	14.0%	5.7%

TABLE III-16: Problems Relating To Indexing And/Or Cataloging Of Microforms

	(N)	Large	Constant but not large	Occasional	Rare	None	Not applicable	No response
Public	(22)	4.5%	9.1%	36.4%	9.1%	9.1%	18.2%	13.6%
Academic	(66)	28.8	10.6	19.7	10.6	22.7	4.5	3.0
Special	(69)	7.2	8.7	14.5	23.2	24.6	17.4	4.3
Total	(157) 100%	15.9%	9.6%	19.7%	15.9%	21.7%	12.1%	5.1%

not applicable and 13 gave no response at all (Table III-17). Libraries offering comments on this issue indicated for the most part that the microform index or catalog is separate from the main catalog. However, two academic institutions said that microforms are cataloged the same as books and are interfiled in the main catalog.

More than one-third of the respondents indicated that they had occasional problems with microform use -- that is, they found that library patrons preferred hard copy to microforms and often resisted using microforms even when they had no other means of obtaining the information. The same percentage reported rare or non-existent problems with microform use,while 20% of the respondents said they encountered either constant or large difficulties here.

One academic library reported a constant but not large problems with "patron apprehension," while another said it also had a constant problem but relied on staff training and user orientation to overcome it. A special librarian reporting occasional problems emphasized that, "Users like hard copy,"and another special librarian who said his problems were constant but not large noted that the situation is "improving each year " (Table III-18).

As might be expected, an overwhelming percentage of libraries reported that they had no problems with microform circulation or that circulation problems did not apply to them. Another six failed to respond to the question (Table III-19). Of those who do circulate microforms, 23 reported only rare problems, with 18 of those indicating that they ran into problems occasionally. Only 15 libraries indicated that they had encountered large or constant problems with circulation. The bulk of the comments on this question were "don't circulate" or "not circulated." However, one library reporting "no problems" explained that, "Since the facilities for reading and printing are here, most patrons use the materials in the library and the lending rate is consequently low. The majority of loans made are interlibrary loans." Another library that does circulate microforms but encountered no problems noted that, "We'll circulate, but user can make hard copy."

Multiple formats and reduction ratios

No special difficulties were reported as a result of multiple formats. Of the 157 respondents, a total of 39% reported rare or no problems; 28% said they had only

TABLE III-17: Problems Relating To Integration Of Index Or Catalog
Information With Main Catalog

	(N)	Large	Constant but not large	Occasional	Rare	None	Not applicable	No response
Public	(22)	4.5%	18.2%	13.6%	18.2%	13.6%	18.2%	13.6%
Academic	(66)	22.7	6.1	13.6	6.1	34.8	10.6	6.1
Special	(69)	4.3	13.0	5.8	14.5	31.9	21.7	8.7
Total	(157) 100%	12.1%	10.8%	10.2%	11.5%	30.6%	16.6%	8.3%

TABLE III-18: Problems Relating To Microform Use

	(N)	Large	Constant but not large	Occasional	Rare	None	Not applicable	No response
Public	(22)	--	13.6%	45.5%	22.7%	4.5%	--	13.6%
Academic	(66)	6.1%	13.6	40.9	18.2	16.7	--	4.5
Special	(69)	11.6	11.6	29.0	27.5	13.0	2.9%	4.3
Total	(157) 100%	7.6%	12.7%	36.3%	22.9%	13.4%	1.3%	5.7%

TABLE III-19: Problems Relating To Microform Circulation

	(N)	Large	Constant but not large	Occasional	Rare	None	Not applicable	No response
Public	(22)	4.5%	4.5%	--	13.6%	9.1%	59.1%	9.1%
Academic	(66)	1.5	9.1	19.7%	13.6	28.8	24.2	3.0
Special	(69)	5.8	2.9	7.2	15.9	33.3	31.9	2.9
Total	(157) 100%	3.8%	5.7%	11.5%	14.6%	28.0%	32.5%	3.8%

occasional problems   (Table III-20).   Twenty-five percent
said they would describe their problems stemming from
multiple formats as large or constant.

Predictably, the least number of problems in this
area were reported by public libraries. The comments
explain why: most of them use only microfilm on reels.
An academic library complained that its fiche attachment
doesn't fit its equipment, while another reporting constant
problems with multiple formats said they were due to file
integrity as far as fiche were concerned and with finding
specific articles or sections on reels. Another academic
library with large problems in this area commented on the
need for standards, while one that said the problem didn't
apply added that, "There would be no problem if all microforms were cataloged." A special library with constant
problems relating to multiple formats had this to say:
"Non-compatibility of equipment is no longer excusable,
manufacturers."

Multiple reduction ratios are proving somewhat more
of a problem. Fifteen percent of the respondents said
they constituted a large problem, while 20% said difficulties were constant but not large   (Table III-21).   Another 22% rated them as occasional. Comments here reflected
a desire for standardization. One academic library said it
did not purchase microforms with large reduction ratios;
another complained that multiple reduction ratios require
"too many pieces of equipment," while still another with
large problems in the area recommended that libraries "decide and adhere to (their) own rules." Special libraries
complained of the need for lens changes to read microforms
of varying reduction ratios. One said it had to decide by
trial and error what lens to use and noted that, "It would
help if vendor showed film reduction." Another complained
that, "British titles mean exceptions -- lenses are too
expensive."

Relatively few librarians found difficulty in obtaining
continuing education about library micrographics. Less than
20% said they encountered large or constant problems in this
area, while 24% said they experienced only occasional difficulties, and 40% said they ran into problems rarely or
not at all   (Table III-22).

One academic librarian who admitted to constant problems in this area noted that, "Keeping up with literature
is especially time-consuming as is training of both staff

TABLE III-20: Problems As A Result Of Multiple Formats

	(N)	Large	Constant but not large	Occasional	Rare	None	Not applicable	No response
Public	(22)	9.1%	18.2%	18.2%	9.1%	36.4%	--	9.1%
Academic	(66)	9.1	16.7	31.8	21.2	19.7	1.5%	--
Special	(69)	10.1	11.6	27.5	10.1	24.6	8.7	7.2
Total	(157) 100%	9.6%	14.6%	28.0%	14.6%	24.2%	4.5%	4.5%

TABLE III-21: Problems Resulting From Multiple Reduction Ratios

	(N)	Large	Constant but not large	Occasional	Rare	None	Not applicable	No response
Public	(22)	22.7%	13.6%	13.6%	13.6%	13.6%	13.6%	9.1%
Academic	(66)	18.2	22.7	18.2	16.7	16.7	6.1	1.5
Special	(69)	10.1	20.3	29.0	14.5	11.6	7.2	7.2
Total	(157) 100%	15.3%	20.4%	22.3%	15.3%	14.0%	7.6%	5.1%

TABLE III-22: Problems Of Obtaining Continuing Education
About Library Micrographics

	(N)	Large	Constant but not large	Occasional	Rare	None	Not applicable	No response
Public	(22)	--	18.2%	31.8%	9.1%	9.1%	13.6%	18.2%
Academic	(66)	6.1%	13.6	21.2	24.2	22.7	3.0	9.1
Special	(69)	4.3	13.0	24.6	20.3	18.8	7.2	11.6
Total	(157) 100%	4.5%	14.0%	24.2%	20.4%	19.1%	6.4%	11.5%

and users." Another dismissed the question with the comment
that, "We must use the equipment we have; this is usually
the infrequent problem of initial or replacement selection."
Only one public librarian commented on this issue, noting
that he had "no time" for continuing education since the
library's resources were so limited. A special librarian
objected to most materials as "too technical for our needs."
Two special librarians who reported only rare problems with
continuing education mentioned several educational sources,
among them trade magazines and journals, "sources in my own
geographic area," and the advice of scientific staff who
attend NMA meetings.

LIBRARY HOLDINGS AND PRACTICES

The second section of the questionnaire focused on
library practices relating to microforms and their use, and
attempted to determine the extent of the responding libraries' microform holdings. As might be expected, microfiche units far outnumbered microfilm holdings among all
types of libraries. The numbers developed by this question
cannot be regarded as statistically significant because of
the nature of the survey itself. However, Table III-23 does
give an indication of how holdings were spread among the
three types of libraries.

TABLE III-23: Microform Holdings

	Academic	Public	Special
Reels			
Mean	23,162	11,278	4,011
Median	13,000	8,226	500
Population	53	16	51
Fiche			
Mean	163,638	58,711	105,560
Median	98,000	1,750	13,000
Population	46	9	56
Users			
Mean			
Median			1000
Population			
High	50,000	2.8 million	50,000
Low	200	40,000	125

Of more value were the findings relating to the circulation of microforms, library purchasing and cataloging
policies, efforts to educate patrons in the use of microforms and microform reading equipment, and resources upon
which librarians rely to keep abreast of developments in
microforms and micrographics.

A surprisingly high percentage of respondents indicated
that they do circulate microforms, although predictably,
most public libraries replied that they do not. Among the
65 academic institutions replying to this part of the survey, most of them (39) said that they do circulate microforms, while 26 indicated that they do not. Slightly more
than half of the special libraries replied that they do
not circulate microforms: 36 librarians said no, while 31
said yes.

In some cases, academic libraries indicated that they
circulate microforms only under unusual circumstances such
as when a patron is ill and unable to use the facilities
in the library. Others noted that circulation was rare or
limited (Table III-24).

TABLE III-24: Circulation Of Microforms
And Lending Of Readers

Circulate Microforms

	(N)	Yes	%	No	%	No response	%
Public	(22)	6	27%	16	73%		
Academic	(65)	39	60	26	40		
Special	(69)	31	45	36	52	2	3%
Total	(156)	76	49%	78	50%	2	1%

Lend Readers

	(N)	Yes	%	No	%	No response	%
Public	(22)	0	0	22	100%		
Academic	(65)	34	52%	31	48		
Special	(69)	30	43	37	54	2	3%
Total	(156)	64	41%	90	58%	2	1%

A related question dealt with the lending of microform readers. On this issue public libraries were unanimous: none loaned readers under any circumstances. However, more than half of the academic libraries reported that they did lend readers. Of the 65 responses, 34 libraries did have a reader lending program, while 31 did not. Special libraries were also evenly divided on the question, with slightly more (37 compared to 30) indicating that they did not lend readers at all.

In comparing responses on the circulation questions, it developed that among academic libraries there were 11 cases where either readers or microforms were lent, but not both by the same institution; within special and government libraries, there were eight instances where either readers or microforms, but not both, were lent. One academic and two special libraries commented that they duplicated microfiche rather than lending them, while a number of academic libraries indicated that they restricted loans to faculty and/or graduate students.

Periodicals on microfilm

More than half of the respondents indicated that they purchased periodical backsets on microfilm as a policy. This was most widespread among public libraries where 18 of 22 respondents answered in the affirmative (Table III-25). Only three said that they did not purchase periodicals on microfilm as a policy, while one did not reply to the question. Among academic and special libraries, slightly more than half of each indicated that they did purchase microfilm backsets as policy. Of the 69 special libraries, 36 said that they did, while 30 said that they did not at present purchase periodical backsets on film as policy. Three said that they planned to do so in the future. A total of 34 of the 65 academic libraries responding to this question said that they do buy microform backsets as policy, while 31 said that they do not. Two of these, however, said that they would be buying microfilm as policy in the future.

TABLE III-25:   Purchase Periodical Backsets
On Microfilm As Policy

	(N)	Yes	%	No	%	No response	%
Public	(22)	18	82%	3	14%	1	4%
Academic	(65)	34	52	31	48		
Special	(69)	36	52	30	43	3	5
Total	(156)	88	56%	64	41%	4	3%

Relatively few of the libraries responding to the survey stated that they presently used a microform catalog. Among public libraries, the negative answers were in the large majority. A total of 16 of the 22 respondents said that they did not use a microform catalog and of those, only seven said that they contemplated doing so in the future (Table III-26). Among academic libraries, a substantial majority -- 60% -- said that they did not now use a microform catalog. Roughly the same proportion of special libraries, 38%, currently use a microform catalog and even fewer said they might do so eventually.

TABLE III-26:   Libraries Using Or Planning
To Use Microform Catalogs

Use A Microform Catalog

	(N)	Yes	%	No	%	No response	%
Public	(22)	6	27%	16	73%		
Academic	(65)	24	37	39	60	2	3%
Special	(69)	26	38	36	52	7	10
Total	(156)	56	36%	91	58%	9	6%

Plan To Use Microform Catalog In The Future

	(N)	Yes	%	No	%	No response	%
Public	(22)	7	32%	9	41%	6	27%
Academic	(65)	21	32	28	43	16	25
Special	(69)	10	14	16	23	43	62
Total	(156)	38	24%	53	34%	65	42%

As might be expected, an overwhelming majority of respondents claimed that they educate library patrons in the use of microform equipment and micropublications. Only four academic and four special libraries said that they do not educate users, while only one public library replied in the negative. However, it specified that it did educate patrons in the use of the equipment but not in the use of micropublications   (Table III-27).

TABLE III-27:   Educate Users Regarding
Microforms

	(N)	Yes	%	No	%	No response	%
Public	(22)	21	96%	1	4%		
Academic	(65)	61	94	4	6		
Special	(69)	60	87	4	6	5	7%
Total	(156)	142	91%	9	6%	5	3%

A related question could be interpreted to indicate how successful libraries have been with their user education programs. It concerned user attitudes toward microforms and asked librarians to indicate whether they thought patrons (1) hated; (2) mildly disliked; (3) were unconcerned with the format; or (4) liked microforms. Here, the largest group indicated that patrons mildly dislike using microforms. A total of 75 out of the 156 responses, or 48%, fell into this category. Nearly one-third, however, said they believed patrons did not care what format they used as long as they obtained the information they were seeking. A total of 48 librarians took this view of user attitudes. Only eight indicated that they believed users like microforms, while 17 said that they had the impression that users hated them. Six failed to reply. (Table III-28)

TABLE III-28:   User Attitudes Toward
Microforms

	(N)	Hate	%	Mildly dislike	%	Don't care	%
Public	(22)	0	0	9	41%	10	45
Academic	(65)	9	14%	31	48	18	28
Special	(69)	8	12	35	51	20	29
Total	(156)	17	11%	75	48%	48	31%

	(N)	Like	%	No response	%
Public	(22)	2	9%	1	4%
Academic	(65)	7	11	-	-
Special	(69)	1	1	5	7
Total	(156)	10	6%	6	4%

The survey also sought to determine what copying charges libraries impose for use of their microform reader/printers and whether or not they were satisfied with the quality of the copies. The most common charge among public libraries was ten cents, although five of them charged 25 cents per copy, and another nine listed charges ranging from nothing at all to $1. On this question, a clear majority -- 13 of the 22 respondents -- said they were satisfied with the quality of the copies, while seven said they were not. Only one library failed to respond to this question.

As might be expected, most special libraries levied no charge at all for use of the reader/printer. Of those that did impose a fee, the most common charge was ten cents. A substantial number indicated that they were satisfied with the quality of the copies -- 35 of 69 respondents gave positive replies here. However, nine said they were dissatisfied, while another 12 librarians noted that the quality of copies varies. Four did not respond at all.

The most common charge for use of reader/printers among academic libraries was ten cents. A total of 36 of the 65 respondents, or 55%, listed this as the charge per page. Only two of them said copies were provided free of charge, while ten said they charged 15 cents per copy, two said they charged only five cents, and three said the usual charge was 25 cents. Another 12 listed fees ranging up to $1. The majority of the academic libraries voiced satisfaction with the quality of the copies -- 42 of the 65 respondents. However, 12 said they were dissatisfied and seven said the quality of copies varies. Here, too, four failed to respond to the question.

In an effort to learn what librarians do to keep abreast of developments in micrographics, they were asked if they had ever attended a National Micrographics Association (NMA) meeting or any other conference or class on microforms/micrographics. Most of the public librarians responding indicated that they never had attended an NMA meeting or a class (Table III-29). Slightly higher percentages were reported by special (28%) and academic librarians (29%), but a majority had not attended an NMA meeting. Almost half of the special librarians, however, reported attending some conference or class on micrographics.

The last question was aimed at ascertaining what publications were used most heavily by librarians in obtaining information on microforms and micrographics. The following seven choices were listed:

(1) The <u>Library Technology Report</u> series;

(2) <u>Microform Review</u>;

(3) "Evaluation of Micropublications: A Handbook for Librarians" by Allen B. Veaner;

(4) "The Invisible Medium" by Francis Spigai;

(5) <u>Journal of Micrographics</u>;

(6) "Introduction to Micrographics" (an NMA publication);

(7) the annual review of developments in micrographics appearing in "Library Resources and Technical Services."

In rating these publications, librarians were asked to indicate whether they were: (1) very useful; (2) somewhat useful; (3) useless; (4) never used. Space was provided for comments.

TABLE III-29: Attendance At NMA Meeting

	(N)	Yes	%	No	%	No response	%
Public	(22)	5	23%	17	77%	-	-
Academic	(65)	19	29	45	69	1	2%
Special	(69)	19	28	48	70	2	2
Total	(156)	43	28%	110	71%	3	2%

Attendance At Micrographics Conference Or Class

	(N)	Yes	%	No	%	No response	%
Public	(22)	4	18%	18	82%	-	-
Academic	(65)	21	32	44	68	-	-
Special	(69)	33	48	32	46	4	6%
Total	(156)	58	37%	94	60%	4	3%

Responses indicated that the most useful publication is Library Technology Reports. Forty-one percent found it very useful, while another 35% rated it as somewhat useful; only 22% had never used it. In evaluating the responses, an attempt was made to determine the extent to which librarians were aware of the seven different resources listed. It was found that 64% of all respondents had used "Library Resources and Technical Services'"annual review of micrographics; 57% has used Microform Review; 53% NMA's "Introduction to Micrographics"; 51% the Journal of Micrographics; 50% Veaner's "Evaluation of Micropublications"; and 33% "The Invisible Medium."

Table III-30 is a breakdown of all respondents ratings of the seven publications. Complaints and comments about them varied. For instance, one academic librarian commented that LTR "could be more critical" while another complained that the same publication "tests dated equipment and needs to be more current." Still another remarked that LTR "never has the latest equipment."

TABLE III-30: Literature Sources

	Very Useful	Somewhat Useful	Useless	Never Used It
Library Technology Reports	59 (41%)*	51 (35%)	3 (2%)	31 (22%)
Microform Review	41 (29%)	39 (28%)	1 (1%)	60 (43%)
"Evaluation of Micropublications"	32 (23%)	36 (26%)	2 (1%)	71 (50%)
"Invisible Medium"	22 (16%)	22 (16%)	1 (1%)	91 (67%)
Journal of Micrographics	21 (15%)	47 (34%)	3 (4%)	68 (49%)
NMA's "Introduction to Micrographics"	20 (15%)	46 (34%)	5 (4%)	64 (47%)
"LR&TS Annual Review"	39 (28%)	49 (35%)	1 (1%)	51 (36%)

*All percentages are based on total number of responses to this particular question, not the total number of responses to the survey as a whole.

In commenting on Veaner's "Evaluation of Micropublications," one academic librarian volunteered that he had "no time to worry about quality" and another seconded that notion by adding that, "It would be more useful if we had staff to implement recommended practices." One academic librarian found the Journal of Micrographics "too technical" as did a second who offered the opinion that Judith Fair's Microform Review series on the microform reading room is "particularly valuable."

Special librarians were far less forthcoming with their comments. One did note that Microform Review's articles are "not pertinent to this library," while another found the NMA's "Introduction to Micrographics" "too elementary."

IV

LIBRARIANS SPEAK OUT

As a supplement to the results of the survey presented in the preceding chapter and to explore the day-to-day problems librarians face in handling their expanding microform collections, a series of informal interviews was conducted, mostly by telephone. Librarians contacted were encouraged to talk "off the top of their heads" about what they see as the pros and cons of microform use and the steps they have taken to resolve any problems they have encountered.

No attempt was made to structure the interviews in order to elicit views on any particular aspect of microforms and their use. It developed, however, that librarians were concerned primarily with two types of problems:

(1) those relating to the adequacy of equipment; and

(2) those related to patron acceptance of microforms.

The most frequently heard complaint was that microform reading equipment has not been developed for heavy library use and that reader/printers are for the most part unreliable and difficult to maintain in good working order. The patron acceptance issue is one that clearly troubles many librarians, who seem willing to take the blame for not creating a positive atmosphere for microform use. However, those who had moved into new facilities with specially designed microform reading rooms reported patron responses ranging from uncomplaining to enthusiastic.

Interview results will be presented in this chapter in much the same sequence as microform problems were reviewed in Chapter II -- beginning with equipment and ending with microform use and patron resistance. (Some of the librarians interviewed specifically requested that they not be identified by name. Those requests have been honored and the librarians in question are referred to only by the type of institution they represent.)

EQUIPMENT

Echoing the perennial complaint that microform reading equipment isn't designed for libraries is a man who has made a "thorough-going commitment to the mass use of micro-forms," T. Gene Hodges, Dean of Library Services at Central State University, Edmund, Okla. The commitment was made ten years ago, Hodges explained, out of the need to "expand our collections in the most rapid and cost-effective manner pos-sible." The university library determined to choose micro-forms, where possible, over hard copy for three reasons:

(1) the initial cost of acquisition;

(2) the storage costs per foot; and

(3) the savings possible in the event of mutilation and/or loss.

Although Hodges reports himself more than satisfied with the concentration on microforms, he is far from happy with the reading equipment available. "Here is where the industry is at its lowest ebb," he says. "Reading machines are de-signed for use by business and industry and by trained users, not for the Oklahoma farm boy who comes here as a student and never has seen microfilm before."

Central State has no motor-driver readers at all- a re-flection of Hodges' conviction that such equipment is "just too complicated -- if you mess it up with fancy gadgets, you've got trouble." The library has 50 rollfilm readers and about 20 fiche readers.

While many of the librarians interviewed shared Hodges' views, one who emphatically did not is Richard Boss of the Princeton University Library. Although Boss concedes that a lot of the reading machines for the library market are not very good, he faulted librarians for failing to properly maintain the equipment they do have and for failing to under-stand its use. Too often, he speculated, librarians do not insist that sales people demonstrate preventive maintenance techniques.

To an extent, he blames manufacturers for the volume of complaints about equipment emanating from the library com-munity. "They try to make the standard model as cheap as possible and often don't tell librarians about the options available to make the equipment more effective."

Other librarians charge that easily understandable instructions don't come with the machines, or, if they do, are not permanently attached and simple enough for inexperienced users to understand. One librarian asserted that even the controls are frequently not obvious. In the library, he added, "If there's a way of doing something wrong, you can be sure it will be done wrong. The average student will misuse it."

Complaints about reader/printers were widespread, confirming a survey finding that this type of equipment is the most problematical. A typical comment was that there are no good coin-operated models and that it is hard to keep the machines in good repair.

Hodges explained that to keep his library's readers in good working order all of them are tested each morning to make sure that light bulbs and manual film-transport handles are operating. Furthermore, a staff member attends repair clinics to learn how to cope with minor malfunctions. Other librarians said they had regular service contracts. But some did complain that they have encountered problems in getting prompt repairs.

Bill Roselle at the University of Wisconsin Library in Milwaukee says his library operates on the rule of thumb that, "We don't want to see an out-of-order sign for more than 24 hours." The library is open 24 hours a day, seven days a week and the microform reading room was one of a handful that Francis Spreitzer rated as "good" during his 1974 survey of 60 libraries. Since out-of-service equipment so often stimulates patron resistance, Roselle emphasizes prompt repairs or removal of the malfunctioning unit from the reading area.

FILM

Although micropublishers have been stepping up efforts to convince librarians that vesicular film is an adequate and cheaper substitute for silver halide film, most of the librarians interviewed indicated that despite the appeal of lower costs, they'll continue to specify silver film in microfilm purchases whenever a choice is offered.

Clearly, librarians are awaiting development of a national standard for non-silver film. Dale Cluff at the University of Utah said that the library is buying ERIC documents in silver now, "even though it is twice as expensive as vesicular." The library made the switch back to silver from vesicular "when we ran into problems duplicating the ERIC fiche....The vesicular was giving unreadable copies," Cluff explained.

Eva Sidhom at New York University's Bobst Library said that although micropublishers are "now singing the praises of other cheaper materials, we have to be very cautious in accepting them until the claims are proven." Where possible, she purchases only silver film.

Two special libraries were less emphatic about the need to specify silver film in their microform purchases. One said that silver is preferred "if there's a choice," while the other said no type of film is specified in purchase orders.

Dean Hodges at Central State University expressed a preference for silver film but maintained that he would readily purchase vesicular or diazo microforms. "When I buy a book," he explained, "I never ask how long it will last. I buy it because I need it. Now although I do want the best film, I don't worry about whether it will last or not. When it wears out or is lost, I can always get a replacement."

As a whole, the librarians interviewed were keenly aware of the lack of national standards for non-silver film and of the ALA recommendation that libraries purchase only silver film until standards for vesicular and diazo are established.

On a related issue, few of the librarians said they were able to do more than an occasional spot check of incoming microforms to make sure that they were getting what they paid for and that the micropublications were clear, in focus, and readable. An exception was Hodges who explained that, "Like book shipments, microform shipments are checked against both the original order and the invoice. Each microfilm reel is collated on a reader, and microfiche is visually inspected for quality and correct identity....Any defective microform or incorrect shipment is returned for rectification."

For the most part, however, librarians said that defects in microforms are discovered only when a user finds that something is missing, out of focus, or otherwise badly photographed. Richard De Gennaro at the University of Pennsylvania Library said that he finds quite a bit of slipshod filming. "I think the sellers are aware that we can't examine all the microforms we receive and (so they) cut corners here and there." Another academic librarian found that the quality of the film "varies tremendously....Some of the best companies do the sloppiest work at times. It happens quite a bit. It's impossible to check everything, especially with foreign language micropublications."

Richard Boss at Princeton disagreed. "We don't have many problems with film from major manufacturers," he asserted. "Most of the difficulties are with film supplied by small organizations."

However, Princeton has no system of quality control or procedure for securing replacements from micropublishers when defective film is discovered. Eventually, said Boss, the library will devise an inspection system for new receipts and alert patrons to report any defects they may come across.

Victor Marx at Central Washington State College in Ellensburg, Washington said that the staff there would have to be doubled to check all incoming microforms. "It's cheaper to claim that a film is missing when you discover that it's missing than at the beginning when it doesn't come in. Of course, this system lets unscrupulous publishers get away with murder."

Most of the librarians interviewed said they return inadequate film when it comes to their attention. For the most part, they expressed satisfaction with micropublishers' responses to complaints.

STANDARDS

One of the most vexing problems for many libraries is that of multiple formats and the need for different kinds of equipment to read them all. John Webb of the Oregon Department of Libraries said that the formats issue is especially troublesome for small libraries. These institutions often have to make a choice between fiche and film because they can afford only one type of reader and because, "There is no good reader that can handle both."

Most academic libraries, of course, do have the equipment for both fiche and film as well as for micro-opaques and ultrafiche. And academic librarians have some definite preferences for one type of microform over another. Eva Sidhom at NYU, for instance, prefers film for most material. "We have a few periodicals on fiche, but I find film superior for periodicals." For reports, such as ERIC, she prefers microfiche. Ben Weil, at Exxon, says he prefers rollfilm for journals, too.

Many librarians like film better simply because it is easier to file than microfiche. Typical of this position

are the views expressed by Victor Marx who says that, "From
a management point of view, (roll) film is preferable
because of file integrity. If you misfile fiche, it's
lost. Film will always turn up."

Mark Yerburgh at the State University of New York at
Albany speculated that fiche is getting more and more popular generally. "It is better for monographs," he says, "while
rollfilm is better for newspapers. Also, fiche is easier to
reproduce."

Out in Milwaukee, Bill Roselle at the University of
Wisconsin Library said he'd like to see more standardization
of microformats and more emphasis on fiche. "Once you get
over the problem of file integrity, there are lots of advantages," he explains. "Fiche is easily duplicated....It
is cheaper to duplicate a fiche than to circulate a book."

Others interviewed expressed no particular preference
for one format over the other, saying only that they buy for
content and seldom have a choice of format. "I'd like to
have them settle on some standards," said one documents librarian, "but we'll still have the old ones."

Allen Veaner, assistant director of the Stanford University Library and editor of Microform Review, speculated
that it would not be before the year 2000 that microforms
would become standardized. Then, he said, three types
probably would prevail: one for newspapers, one for books,
and a third for technical reports.

BIBLIOGRAPHIC CONTROL

Predictably, the academic librarians interviewed were
the ones most concerned about access to microforms, particularly to large, multi-volume sets. This issue was not
regarded as a significant problem by the librarians at
public or special institutions.

The access problem is Eva Sidhom's number one gripe.
"There is a poverty of guides and access tools and bibliographies and indexes....Most micropublishers have shown a
lack of interest in this area." Mark Yerburgh said that,
ideally, catalog cards should accompany micropublications
"as if the microforms were books on the shelf."

Although the academic librarians interviewed agreed
on the need for more and better bibliographic controls which

they felt should be provided by the micropublishers, there was some disagreement as to whether microforms should be treated the same as books for cataloging purposes. Most agreed that the fact that information is contained on microfilm rather than in a book should make no difference from a cataloging point of view. But a few took the position that libraries just can't afford to give the full catalog treatment to everything.

Some get around the problem by avoiding the purchase of sets that don't include full bibliographic tools. Others conceded that, practically speaking, cataloging microforms as if they were books just isn't being done. "There's a resistance in the catalog department to the cataloging of non-print materials," explains Dale Cluff. Adds Boss, "There's a prejudice in favor of hard copy. We're now wrestling with the problem of how we can change priorities so that cataloging can be based on the material."

For the most part, the librarians interviewed seemed to agree that the obvious solution to the problem is insistence that micropublishers provide more and better bibliographic controls -- specifically catalog cards rather than book or other cumulative printed indexes. Although they recognize that microform sets will cost more with extensive controls, librarians seemed resigned to the economic burden. No one suggested that individual libraries undertake the cataloging of extensive sets except, possibly, via cooperative arrangements.

USER RESISTANCE

Without exception, the librarians interviewed were concerned about the acceptance of microforms by library patrons. In general, they seemed to agree that users' attitudes stem directly from the attitude of the person serving them. Several described the efforts they had made to encourage use of microforms. Eva Sidhom, who moved into a brand new reading room designed specifically for the use of microforms, sees the setting as ideal. "We have custom-made carrels, modern readers, two reader/printers, and we haven't had any equipment problems. This room was designed to provide the proper atmosphere to make the use of microforms agreeable. We give readers assistance with the machines even though there are printed instructions attached to each one. This is one place where reader attitudes have been transformed because a well-planned and well-thought out facility has been provided."

Just to prove her point, Sidhom asked patrons to respond to a questionnaire aimed at determining attitudes toward microforms. The results were overwhelmingly favorable. A total of 54% said that microfilm did not bother their eyes, while only 5% said it did. Another 23 "strongly disagreed" with the notion that it could bother the eyes, while 28% agreed that it could. Of those polled, 55% said the advantages of microforms outweighed the disadvantages. After the new library opened, Sidhom reported a "substantial increase" in microform use compared to previous years in the old facility.

Boss at Princeton turned up these seven specific complaints when he sought to determine why students and faculty disliked using microforms:

(1) The physical area where the microforms were available was unattractive, almost "dungeon-like."

(2) The light level was poor. In general, there was too little light.

(3) The equipment was old, outmoded, and in short supply. It also was poorly maintained.

(4) The hours of service in the microform room were inadequate and the room was not well staffed.

(5) The staff was not properly trained to handle microforms.

(6) Material on microforms was not cataloged.

(7) Material on microforms couldn't be circulated while equivalent materials in hard copy could be.

Princeton is now in the process of upgrading its equipment, and putting some members of the library staff through training programs designed to improve their knowledge of microforms and their handling. Boss is convinced that the principal reason for the negative attitude toward microforms on the part of faculty and students is the negative experiences they have had with the library's facilities. "In large part it could have been avoided. But I don't think librarians have been committed to making microforms a successful medium. We have provided a bad environment, inadequate staff; we don't process the materials, don't update the equipment, and don't service the equipment."

Elizabeth Gibson, the librarian at Merrill, Lynch, Pierce, Fenner and Smith tried to head off complaints about the introduction of microforms by asking staff members who would be using microfiche extensively to help select the equipment. "We had a voting sheet on the readers before we made any purchases," she explained. "We didn't buy on a price basis. We selected the reader that people here preferred after they had a chance to see what was available."

Some of the investment analysts at Merrill, Lynch persisted in asking for hard copies of the 10K and other reports corporations are required to file with the Securities and Exchange Commission; the Merrill, Lynch library buys these reports from Disclosure, Inc. But the firm is so committed to its "fiche only" policy that microforms prevailed for these reports despite some initial grumbling from the analysts. Each one has a fiche reader on his desk.

Other special libraries have other means of encouraging microform use. Exxon, for instance, doesn't tell users whether the publication they are seeking is in a bound volume or on film. "We only use microfilm in cartridges and we have no readers, only reader/printers. If it's on film, it goes right on the reader/printer and once he (the user) finds it, he can print it. We've never had a murmur," explains Exxon's Ben Weil.

At the University of Utah, Dale Cluff insists that, "User resistance is a myth. It comes out of the tradition of dark rooms and no one available to help. Here, we put the staff out there to be outgoing, to extend themselves and volunteer help and information so that the patron doesn't mind using microforms."

At the University of Wisconsin in Milwaukee, the microform reading room is one of the stops on the student orientation tour. It's a new facility opened in 1974 and, reports librarian Bill Roselle, "We've had a good reaction to it." The room is constantly staffed and the library itself never closes.

Roselle believes that the younger the user, the less resistance to microforms. "There's a different breed of cat coming to college today," he explained. "Most of them have a background of upwards of 15,000 hours of different kinds of educational technology. They've used readers, television, computer terminals, videotapes. The kids today are more sophisticated. The people who grouse about using microforms

are the senior faculty, not the graduate students and certainly not the undergraduates."

Mark Yerburgh at the State University of New York at
Albany shares that view. "The older faculty members show
resistance, but even that is changing now because so much
information is available only on microform."

Nevertheless, most of the librarians interviewed were
of the opinion that no one really likes to use microfilm and
that they, too, prefer hard copy to this "medium once re-
moved." But given the fact that so much information today
is available and affordable only on microform, they seemed
committed to making microforms work. The stumbling block,
of course, is money and the limited financial resources of
most libraries to upgrade microform facilities in older institutions.

THE FUTURE

In addition to the five problems discussed above, it
became clear in the course of the interviews that many librarians are looking toward the future with new interest
in the savings and conveniences microforms have to offer.
Harold Schleifer, acquisitions librarian at New York City's
Lehman College, suggests that a valuable service would be
microform summaries of upcoming scientific journal articles
that could be distributed in advance of actual journal publication. "There's such a long delay from the time an
article is accepted for publication and the time it actually
appears," he explains. "These delays are a disservice to
the academic community. If journals would publish a summary version, individual subscribers would be able to keep
up with current studies. Of course, micropublishers would
have to do this on a service-fee basis or some such arrangement. But I think it's worth investigation."

Schleifer participated in the recent R.R. Bowker Co.
comparative feasibility study of "Books in Print" on microfiche versus hard copy and reported, in a Microform Review
article, that the experiment "firmly established" the ef-
fectiveness of the fiche. After a six-month pilot program
-- from December 1974 to June 1975 -- he and his staff
found that microfiche proved to be more efficient than hard
copy searches of "Books in Print" and "Forthcoming Books."
The quickest searches, Schleifer found, were accomplished
when fiche was used for searching entries in random sequence as they occurred within a random batch. "Contrary to
our original expectations," he explained, "it was not at all

necessary to modify our BIP search routines so as to accomodate the fiche format." As a result of the success of the pilot test, he concluded, "we definitely would choose to replace both hard copy BIP and FB with microfiche, but only if the microfiche editions are made available to us at reduced prices."

Although saving space has been highly touted as a reason to replace hard copy with microfilm at least one special librarian voiced doubts that the substitution of microforms for bound back issues of periodicals would be economical from that point of view if the cost of film continues to rise.

Another special librarian said that at present hard copy is being kept even when a microfilm copy of back issues of journals is available. Despite the savings possible in terms of binding costs and the cost of space, the library is, for now, "leery of dumping the hard copy."

Dale Cluff stressed the need for well-trained staff to handle microforms. "I'm more and more convinced that we need a hybrid...someone who is a good reference librarian and also good on micrographics. I think we're going to have to set up criteria for hiring, try to build a job description so that we can get a staff qualified to help ease the reluctance of patrons to use microfilm."

As far as keeping up with developments in micrographics is concerned, most of the librarians interviewed said they found Microform Review especially helpful and most of them also mentioned Library Technology Reports as essential to the equipment selection process. However, a majority seemed to feel that the best way to keep informed is through frequent contact with experts in the field. This informal exchange of views and information -- a grapevine approach to problem-sharing and solving -- was mentioned frequently by librarians like Cluff who have taken a leadership role in the articulation of problems. Names like Allen Veaner, Francis Spreitzer, Alan Meckler, and Cluff cropped up often when librarians talked about microforms and approaches to the problems they present.

Without a doubt the interviews demonstrated a keen awareness of the problems presented by the proliferation of microforms in the library and of the steps being taken to resolve them. However, many of those interviewed -- particularly those who had assumed some leadership in the field -- voiced doubts that the library community as a whole grasped the importance of the controversy regarding the substitution

of vesicular for silver halide film. On the issue of patron
resistance to the use of microforms, many cited Spreitzer's
study and expressed conviction that as a whole, librarians
haven't yet come to terms with their responsibility to encourage microform use. This could be done, they suggested,
by creating the proper atmosphere and insisting that staff
members volunteer explanations and instructions to help
overcome the hesitation of inexperienced users.

V

CONCLUSION

Although microforms still represent a relatively small percentage of total library holdings, they have made substantial gains in the past ten years. The decade has seen a steady improvement in both micrographics technology and in the amount of information available on microforms. For the library, the incentive to invest in microforms was obvious: they cost less than the equivalent information in hard copy. Indeed, the cost factor has far surpassed space saving and preservation of deteriorating materials as libraries' primary reason for acquiring microforms.

By 1976, however, it appears that the microfilm "boom" is over, at least temporarily. Libraries caught in budget squeezes are unable to increase their spending on microforms despite the cost savings they offer. And if John Dessauer is right in his projections of future library acquisitions (see Chapter II), it appears that by 1980, libraries will be spending much more for microforms than they were in 1972-73 -- and receiving fewer units.

Money isn't the only problem libraries face in expanding their microform collections. Clearly, librarians are becoming increasingly sophisticated about what microforms can and cannot offer and very much attuned to the problems presented by increasing reliance on microforms as conveyors of information. These problems fall in two broad areas: hardware -- or the equipment necessary to read microforms -- and software, the micropublications themselves.

HARDWARE PROBLEMS

A review of the results of the survey and interviews conducted in connection with this report demonstrates that hardware problems rank first among librarians' microform concerns. The complaint that there is no suitable microform reading equipment specifically designed for the library was repeated so frequently that it cannot be easily dismissed.

Indeed, the survey results showed that more than half of the librarians who responded were dissatisfied with all types of reading equipment. Reader/printers presented the largest problems with a wide majority --83%* -- reporting that they had problems ranging from "occasional" to "large" with their reader/printers. Another 70% indicated that the use of reader/printers presented problems at least some of the time. While improvements in reader/printers are sure to come someday, experts in the field are reluctant to predict just when. Present day equipment with its reliance on liquid chemicals for the duplication process is clearly a nuisance. The chemicals have to be replenished regularly and, with frustrating frequency, produce damp, curling, and misshapen copies. The only reader/printers offering a dry reproduction process are prohibitively expensive for most libraries.

Complaints about microform readers also are widespread. Sixty-three percent of those responding to a question about the quality of microfilm readers said they had problems at least occasionally. And 58% of those answering the survey question on the quality of microfiche readers indicated that they had problems ranging from occasional to large. Some librarians remain convinced that newer fiche and film readers are inferior to older models, as indicated by the exercise of designing an ideal microfilm reader at the June 1975 ALA conference (see Chapter II). There is widespread agreement on what such a reader should offer: the capability of handling both fiche and rollfilm, a wide range of magnification ratios, durability, and compact size. Unfortunately, librarians do not have the several thousand dollars per reader that such a piece of equipment would cost.

The selection of microfilm reading equipment remains a knotty problem for many libraries. Survey results showed that 66% of the respondents faced at least occasional problems in this area. Reviewing aids such as Library Technology Reports do provide independent information. However, librarians still seem uncomfortable with the specifications and purchase of micrographics equipment, and this in turn hampers the development of full microform utilization programs.

_____

*All percentage figures based on survey results and used in this concluding chapter were calculated by adding together figures representing responses indicating "occasional," "constant but not large," and "large" problems.

While hardware problems are of concern to all librarians, not all of the "software" issues are as broadbased. These fall into four categories: standards, bibliographic control, film, and reader resistance.

MICROPUBLICATIONS: FORMATS, ACQUISITIONS

Although more and more librarians are now willing to acknowledge that different microform formats are necessary to accomodate different types of information, there remains a demand for some standards -- some move to stem the flow of different types of microforms with varying reduction ratios, many of which demand reading equipment that cost-conscious libraries simply cannot afford. Estimates that it will take another 25 years before formats settle down are small comfort to librarians who now must accept or reject new microforms on the basis of whether or not they already have -- or can afford to purchase -- the appropriate reading equipment. More than half the librarians responding to the survey indicated that they have at least occasional problems as a result of multiple formats and multiple reduction ratios.

One trend that has emerged clearly by 1976 is the approaching demise of micro-opaques. Dissatisfaction with micro-opaque readers is widespread and the inadequacy of reader/printers for these microforms is commonly acknowledged. The fact that only 67 of 157 survey respondents were able to answer a question on the quality of micro-opaque readers confirmed that use of this format is on the wane. Among those who did reply, 78% reported that they experienced at least occasional problems with the equipment. As noted in Chapter II, the decision to phase out the purchase of micro-opaques in the California State University and College libraries is a reflection of the discontent with this format and the hardware produced to accommodate it.

The CSUC standards are the most obvious indication that there is a move afoot to put a lid on the acquisition of varying microformats. And the decisions to favor 35mm film over 16mm, to phase out the purchase of micro-opaques, and to limit fiche purchases to those with reduction ratios up to 48X are clear challenges to micropublishers to limit future offerings to formats for which there is widely available reading equipment.

To be sure, not all librarians are willing to take such a firm stand. Many have no preference for one format

over another and some feel that they really have no choice
at all -- they must purchase the format in which the information they need is available. The formats issue is
one that probably will be fought out between academic and
research libraries and micropublishers. Most public library microform collections are limited to back issues of
newspapers and periodicals, and most special libraries
restrict their holdings to specific journals and government publications readily available on the NMA standard
fiche or on 16 or 35mm rollfilm. The crunch will come in
the academic sector as more and more scholarly works are
offered on microforms and new and different formats are
devised to handle the enormous variety of page and print
sizes in which these works were originally published.

For now, academic libraries seem to be evidencing
considerable skepticism toward purchase of the large microform sets, running to thousands of volumes, that were introduced in the late 1960s and early 1970s by such publishers as Library Resources, Inc., an Encyclopaedia
Britannica affiliate. Some of these collections required
special readers; all had high price tags which took money
away from purchase of other materials.

The drying up of demand for these collections is one
illustration of the fact that while the quantity of material on microfilm has expanded greatly in the past decade,
the type of material has changed little. Micropublishing
is still limited primarily to back issues of newspapers
and periodicals, a few specialized kinds of government
documents (NTIS reports, ERIC reports, the SEC filings of
corporations), and the rare research collection available
only on microfilm. With very few exceptions, new books
and current periodical issues are not published in microfilm. (The Pergamon journals would be one of the exceptions.) Nor is there any appreciable demand for such
original micropublications, judging from our interviews
and surveys of libraries.

Beyond the narrow question of format, academic libraries have a continuing problem in their search for more
and better bibliographic controls for microforms. Here
again, costs are at the heart of the dilemma: the libraries
don't have the resources themselves to provide the bibliographic controls so urgently needed with microform sets or
with newspapers and periodicals on microforms. At the same
time they resist the added costs charged by micropublishers
who do include bibliographic controls. Some efforts are
being devoted to explore the possibility of cooperative

library approaches to cataloging microforms, but so far
with little results.

Without a doubt the "access" problem accentuated by
less than adequate cataloging contributes to another
microform concern -- the resistance of library patrons
to using microforms. As noted earlier, this resistance
appears to be somewhat age-related, with older library
users, particularly faculty members, demonstrating the
most reluctance. Younger, more "hardware oriented" users
are more receptive to microforms. Both our interviews
and our survey confirm the presence of an age factor in
user resistance and also indicate that librarians have
become conscious of their own responsibility for the problem. The survey finding that 64 of 146 respondents faced
at least occasional problems with the design and improvement of the reading area indicates that librarians have
become acutely aware of the degree to which dingy and
inconvenient microform reading rooms contribute to user
resistance. The positive responses of library patrons
reported by institutions which have modernized their
microform reading room facilities lend further weight
to the notion that the comfort of the surroundings goes
a long way to weaken reader resistance.

From all indications, user resistance to microforms
today stems largely from the inconvenience of the medium
rather than from technological imperfection. In other
words, better quality film and more sophisticated film
preparation and processing have overcome complaints that
reading microforms is hard on the eyes, a common gripe
in earlier years. True, there continue to be complaints
about out-of-focus or poorly photographed materials and
missing sections. In some cases, as one librarian put
it, micropublishers are "getting away with murder" because they realize that few libraries have the staff and
facilities to carefully inspect all incoming microforms.
New and better quality control programs are the only way
libraries are going to be able to insure that they are
getting what they pay for, although most librarians
participating in the interviews and the survey did not
find quality control to be a major problem. The attitude
seemed to be that few problems arose with materials provided by the major micropublishers and that only occasional
problems arise when dealing with smaller vendors.

Of all the issues related to microforms, the one that
has generated the most controversy is related to the film

itself -- the attempt to replace silver halide with **vesi-cular** film. Librarians are being barraged with two opposing and equally persuasive arguments. On one side are micro-publishers who are attempting to convince libraries that vesicular film is durable and of sufficiently good quality for "use" copies, and that libraries are wasting their money by insisting on silver halide film for materials that are not archivally stored. The cost argument is an attractive one, especially when a micropublisher offers the inducement of a replacement should a vesicular microform fail to live up to the claims made for it.

The other side of the argument is advanced by experts in the field, particularly by Allen B. Veaner, editor of <u>Microform Review</u>, who contends that libraries who buy vesi-cular film before national testing standards are established are essentially buying a pig in a poke. His argument is backed by the ALA recommendation that libraries specify in their microfilm orders that they will accept only silver halide film. The replacement inducement advanced by micro-publishers hasn't persuaded Veaner that vesicular film is worth a try before the testing standards are established. He fears that the micropublishers making such offers may not be around in the future to deliver on their replacement orders. In rebuttal, it could be argued that even a major micropublisher could go out of business or merge with an-other company unwilling to adopt its policies. As with books from major publishers, a title that goes out of print cannot be replaced if it is destroyed, lost, or stolen. And as far as film is concerned, even silver halide de-teriorates with use -- there's no guarantee that a library can get a replacement for a worn out silver halide micro-film if the micropublisher isn't around to provide the substitute.

No immediate resolution of the vesicular vs. silver film controversy seems imminent in view of the long-range studies aimed at developing testing standards. Undoubtedly, some libraries will decide that the lower cost of vesicular film is worth the risk that it may not live up to the claims made for it. But in so doing, prudent libraries will hedge their bets by verifying that a replacement copy would be obtainable should the film in fact deteriorate.

COM CATALOGS AND THE FUTURE

As has been noted earlier, the impact of microforms on libraries goes far beyond the acquisition of books and periodicals. An increasing reliance on COM catalogs and on COM for internal recordkeeping is an obvious application of microforms in the library of the future. Certainly COM is an economically feasible alternative to other forms of automated catalogs. The success of COM catalogs in the relatively few libraries who already have made the switch will prove a positive inducement to other institutions to adopt microfilm as a replacement for cumbersome card catalogs. From the users' point of view, the catalog is a place to look up isolated facts, not to do extended reading, so there should be no strong objections to the microformat, provided there are enough readers available. So far, experience with COM-produced catalogs is so limited that few problems have yet emerged. From all indications, COM appears to offer an efficient and economical alternative for all but the largest and most heavily used public and research libraries.

It would be ironic, but not necessarily unfortunate, if after all the attention devoted to microforms as an alternative to hard copy, the biggest contribution of microfilm in libraries turned out to be not as a replacement for books and journals but as an information management tool in mixed computer/microfilm/paper handling systems. While continuing on the lookout for ways to acquire materials in microform that will satisfy user needs and save the library money, librarians would therefore be well advised to pay attention to the significant role that computer-output-microfilm can play in the organization and cataloging of the library's holdings.

APPENDIX: TEXT OF QUESTIONNAIRE ON MICROFORMS

The following is a list of problems librarians encounter in their attempts to provide library users with books, serials, and reports in microform. Please check the type of library you currently work in: academic____, public____, school____, special____, other (please explain)____.

Rank each of the problems listed below according to your current experience.

	Large Problem	Constant but not large	Occasional problem	Rarely a problem	No Problem	Not Applicable	Comments and/or your solution to the problem
EQUIPMENT							
Microform equipment selection							
Complexity of equipment							
Equipment maintenance							
Quality of microfilm readers							
Quality of microfiche readers							
Quality of micro-opaque readers							
Quality of microform reader/printers (R/P)							
Use of microform readers or R/P's							
Mechanism for microform equipment purchase							
Storage Conditions:							
a. Adherence to standards for archival quality							
b. Integration of microform collection with 'main' collection							
c. Suitable containers, file cabinets, etc.							
Microform reading area design or improvement							
MICROPUBLICATIONS							
Microform acquisition							
Microform quality							
Microform quality control							
Indexing and/or cataloging of microforms							
Integration of index or catalog information with 'main' catalog							
Microform use							
Microform circulation							
Multiple formats (e.g., reel, fiche)							
Multiple reduction ratios (e.g., 24X, 18X, 90X)							
CONTINUING EDUCATION							
Obtaining continuing education about library micrographics							
OTHER							

How many users/patrons does your library have? Potential _____ and/or actual _____. What was last year's book circulation for your library? _____.

How many reels of microfilm _____, microfiches _____, and/or micro-opaque readers _____ does your library own?

How many microfilm reader/printers (R/P's) _____, microfiche R/P's _____, and/or micro-opaque R/P's _____ does your library own

Do you circulate microform? Yes _____ No _____. Do you lend microform readers? Yes _____ No _____.

Do you purchase periodical backsets on microform as a policy? Yes _____ No _____.

Do you use a microform catalog? Yes _____ No _____. Are you contemplating the future use of a micro-form catalog? Yes _____ No _____.

Do you educate library users/patrons to the use of microform equipment and micropublications? Yes _____ No _____.

Do you feel most library users/patrons _____ hate to use microform; _____ mildly dislike using microform; _____ don't care what format they use, but are more concerned with the content; _____ like using micro-form?

What do you charge for R/P copies of microform pages? _____. Is the quality satisfactory? Yes _____ No _____.

Have you ever attended a National Microfilm Association meeting? Yes _____ No _____. Have you attended any conference session, class, etc. on microform/micrographics recently? Yes _____ No _____. Approx. date _____.

Please rate the following literature sources:

	Very Useful	Somewhat Useful	Useless	Never Used It	Comments
LIBRARY TECHNOLOGY REPORTS					
MICROFORM REVIEW (Periodical)					
Allen Veaner's "Evaluation of Micropublications; a Handbook for Librarians"					
F. Spigai's "Invisible Medium"					
JOURNAL OF MICROGRAPHICS (Periodical)					
Nat'l. Microfilm Assn.'s "Introduction to Micrographics"					
LIBRARY RESOURCES & TECHNICAL SERVICES					
"Spring Annual Review of Developments in Library Reprographics"					

Other Comments:

SELECTED BIBLIOGRAPHY (In Order of Citation)

California State University and Colleges. "Revised Microform Procurement Standards," Microform Review, Vol. 4, No. 2. pp. 96-99. April 1975.

American Library Association. Library Technology Reports, November 1975.

"New Equipment Reviewing Service," Microform Review, Vol. 5 No. 1, pp. 8-9. January 1976.

Spaulding, Carl M. "Report of the Chairman of the Library Relations Committee Concerning a SIG for Librarians in the National Microfilm Association," Microform Review, Vol. 4, No. 1. January 1975, pp. 10-12.

Spreitzer, Francis F. "Developments in Copying, Micrographics, and Graphic Communications, 1972," Library Resources and Technical Services. Vol. 17, No. 2. Spring 1973.

Bierman, Kenneth J. "Automated Alternatives to Card Catalogs: The Current State of Planning and Implementation," Journal of Library Automation, Vol. 8/4, December 1975, pp. 277-293

National Reprographic Centre for documentation. "A Proposal to Investigate Methods of Determining the Storage Life of Diazo and Vesicular Microfilms," Microform Review, Vol. 4, No. 2, April 1975, pp. 92-95.

Veaner, Allen B. "An Ominous Trend?/Part III," Microform Review, Vol. 5, No. 1, p.5, January 1976.

Hawken, William R. "Systems Instead of Standards," Library Journal, Sept. 15, 1973.

Veaner, Allen B. "The Crisis in Micropublication," Choice 5 (June 1968): 448-453.

Veaner, Allen B. The Evaluation of Micropublications. Chicago: Library, Technology Program, American Library Association, 1971.

American National Standards Institute. "Standard for the Advertisin of Micropublications," Microform Review, Vol. 4, No. 3, July 1975, pp. 177-179.

Diaz, Albert James. "Microform Information Sources: Publications and Hardware," Microform Review, Vol. 4, No. 4, October 1975, pp. 250-261.

Dessauer, John P. "Library Acquisitions: A Look Into the Future," Publisher's Weekly, June 1975.

Cluff, Dale R. "Determining National Interest and/or Activity Relating to Bibliographic Access of Microforms," Microform Review, Vol. 4, No.4, October 1975, pp. 267-269.

Wooster, Harold. Microfiche 1969--A User Survey. AD 695-049 (Arlington, Va.: Air Force Office of Scientific Research, 1969).

Kottenstette, James P. and Dailey, K. Anne. An Investigation of the Environment for Educational Microform Utilization, Phase II Student Use of Classroom Microform in Support of a Content Course. ED 050-603 (Washington, D.C.: U.S. Office of Education, 1971).

Advanced Technology/Libraries "Spreitzer Criticizes Librarians' Attitude Toward Microforms," Vol. 4, No. 10, October 1975.

Schleifer, Harold B. and Adams, Peggy A. "Books in Print on Microfiche: A Pilot Test," Microform Review Vol. 5, No. 2. April 1976.

INDEX

1759